Build It with Dad

A. J. Hamler

Contents

Outdoor Living

Indoor Living

Introduction

Working with Kids

One of the fondest memories of my daughter Courtney was the day we bought her first "big girl" bed. As I was assembling it, her understandable excitement was eclipsed only by her fascination with the process. She asked tons of questions about what I was doing, and every time I did something new came the plea, "Can I try it, Daddy?"

There really wasn't much I thought she could do, though – the parts were heavy, the assembly complicated, and the tools unfamiliar. She wasn't quite three years old, but she kept asking. Then, when I had one corner of the frame finished, it occurred to me that tightening a couple screws might be a task that was easy enough for her. So I backed off the screws a bit, showed her where each screw was and how the screwdriver fit the end, and told her to go at it.

I needn't have worried. She immediately grasped the concept and after a few moments of fumbling with the screwdriver, she handily took care of it. Her little muscles couldn't tighten it all the way, of course, but I didn't tell her that. Instead, we moved on to the next corner and I let her do all the screws there. Her concentration was such that she didn't even notice me coming behind her to fully tighten screws and bolts. To attach the headboard I first set the bolts and while she held the headboard upright I tightened one side, then we traded places and she took care of the other.

When the bed was complete she was pleased nearly to bursting with her work. In truth, at only three years old her contributions were minimal, but to her mind *she built that bed*, and for months afterward proudly showed it off to every person that came into our house. Not sure I realized it at the time, but I kindled a very important spark that day. In the years that followed, the two of us made a lot of things together in my shop and around the house.

I enjoy building things; always have. But when working with my daughter I realized something else: I enjoyed it even more, and so did she. More importantly, she remembered everything I showed her, and every skill she learned.

Courtney's in her early 30s now, but has continued her interest in building things to this day. In the last year alone she's made her own rustic deck furniture from 200-year-old reclaimed oak, lined a hallway with built-in bookcases, created storage shelves for my new grandson's room, and is currently remodeling a bathroom from the floor up, including tile work, cabinetry, new drywall, flooring and shelves. I couldn't be more proud of her.

Working with kids – what to expect

I'm guessing you've already gotten a taste of this experience and are eager for more, and that's where this book comes in. The 22 projects that follow are perfect for building as a team. I've carefully chosen the projects to represent a wide range of interests. Some are strictly for fun and games, others for those interested in the great outdoors, and some that are useful around the house.

In all cases, though, I've kept things on the simpler side; if there were two ways of doing a particular step or process, the projects typically go with the easier one. I've also geared everything presented here to a basic tool kit. You won't need any large machinery for any of the projects. That's not to say, however, that if you've got a fully tricked-out shop that machinery is off-limits. To the contrary, if there are some steps you'd like to do yourself to save time then, by all means, do that. I'll even note from time to time steps that can be done with larger machines, but it's important to know at the outset that not a single project in this book requires them.

I'm going to assume that you already have a grasp of basic tools and carpentry techniques, so this book isn't a cover-to-cover tutorial on how to become a woodworker. However, when it comes to how a tool works or how something is done I won't leave you hanging; even if you're familiar with the process, I've presented the projects as learning experiences for both you and your young woodworkers.

Keep in mind just how much youngsters will be able to do for themselves and which parts are best left to your adult hands. Unfortunately there's no hard-and-fast rule for this; you'll have to trust your own knowledge of how your kids handle tasks. As you get started, always remember to demonstrate each new technique before you turn them loose, and go slow with things that are new to them. If you see that something is too complicated or a tool too difficult to handle at first, it's imperative that you don't force the child to do it until they have enough confidence to do it safely and in a manner that makes them feel good about the task they've just done.

If you'll be working with more than one child on a project, be sure to keep everyone fully involved. While one is working on the main task, have the other in a support role. Then on the next task they can switch roles. As always, keep age differences in mind: One child may be more ready for a task than the other, or one may tire more quickly.

For groups of three or more, it might be best to have them each work on their own project rather than work together on a single one. This way no one is idle while the others are having fun, and you'll find it easier directing a group on the same task as opposed to dividing your attention among individual kids. Also, by working in this manner each child is at the same step at the same time, everyone gets the same amount of instruction and guidance, and they all finish together. As a bonus, you'll find when working side-by-side on identical projects that they tend to support each other as they work – often without being coached to do so. Don't be surprised to see one child who grasps a task more readily offering help to the others.

It's true that we all learn by trial and error, and there's nothing wrong with a youngster coming away from a task feeling, "I'll do it better next time." But to build confidence and skill it's also important that kids experience doing something correctly. If you see that they're having too much difficulty with something, suggest that you take care of that step yourself while they handle another part of the building process that might be more familiar. Given time and practice, even those difficult tasks will become easier, but you don't want to overload them with things that just don't go right. Above all, it's your job to ensure that everything is done safely.

Safety First

Woodworking can be dangerous, which is why there's a safety warning posted on the copyright page of this (and every) woodworking book. Although a lot of being safe in a woodworking or do-it-yourself environment comes down to common sense and simply paying attention, there are a number of specific safety practices that should be adhered to at all times. I'll emphasize safety tips throughout this book for specific tasks and procedures as they're taking place in the projects, but let's take a look at a few things before we go any further.

Eye protection – the most important rule

First and foremost, protect your eyes and your kids' eyes from sawdust and debris with safety glasses. Since I have to wear glasses anyway, I always get my lenses in a shatterproof material – any time I head to the shop my eyes are already protected – but not a lot of kids wear glasses. Before you do anything else, buy your young woodworker several pairs of safety glasses so there's never an excuse for not being able to find a pair. These glasses come in varying sizes, including sizes for kids. Buy them, and have the children wear them, every time they are in the workshop.

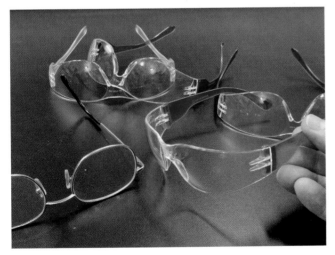

Safety glasses are a must when working with tools and kids need to wear them whenever they are in the workshop. My regular prescription glasses (left) have shatterproof lenses for protection. Inexpensive safety glasses for kids often come in bright colors they'll love to wear.

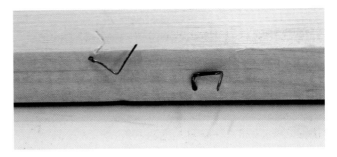

Standard off-the-rack lumber from your local home center may have sharp staples in the board edges—lots of them! To avoid a nasty cut, remove these with pliers as soon as you see them.

Just about everything is sharp

To work effectively, any tool that cuts or drills wood must be sharp. In general, handle tools with respect, avoiding direct contact with cutting edges at all times. When sawing, whether with a handsaw or jigsaw, keep hands away. The same goes for chisels, planes and utility knives. If you have any doubts about your child's ability to handle a sharp tool, then simply don't allow it – do that task yourself until you're confident your child is ready.

To minimize danger when working with tools – sharp or otherwise – workpieces should be securely clamped to a bench or other steady worksurface whenever possible. Things are easier to work with when they're not shifting around, plus clamping a workpiece adds layers of safety:

- Kids simply aren't as strong as we are, and may not be physically able to hold a workpiece steadily and safely. Clamps eliminate this problem.
- The child won't have to divide attention between the tool and holding the workpiece. All concentration can be focused on the task.
- The danger of a workpiece suddenly shifting, causing a correspondingly sudden movement of a cutting tool, is eliminated.
- Strategically placed clamps can act as safety boundaries. Instruct kids never to get a free hand closer than the placement of the clamp.

The sharp edges and tips of tools aside, there are a few other "sharps" you might not expect. One in particular seems to have popped up only in recent years: staples in lumber. Price stickers can fall off, so home centers now staple price tags and barcodes on the ends of lumber. Remove these as soon as you get the material home. If it was just one price tag per board that would be

HAND SAFETY

Eye protection is passive protection. That is, it's something children can wear while doing other things. Once they have safety glasses in place there's nothing else they need to do for the glasses to do their job. Hands are very different because no matter what the woodworking task is, hands are always active. As such, it's imperative they be kept out of the way of anything sharp. Let's take a look at three important ways to keep hands busy, but safe, at all times.

One tool, two hands

While not a hard-and-fast rule, keeping two hands on the tool enhances safety. For a heavy tool that tends to vibrate – like a jigsaw – using both hands not only helps control the cut, it gives the non-dominant hand something to do and, more importantly, somewhere to be. Tools large enough for two-handed use often have a spot that's perfect for resting the hand, as shown here.

Even when the tool isn't heavy, as in the case of this small drill/driver, a second hand helps keep the tool vertically aligned for efficient drilling. And, again, it keeps the non-dominant hand busy and out of harm's way.

Set a strict boundary

Two-handed use shouldn't be mandatory, however, if the action or standing position doesn't lend itself naturally to such hand placement. Many tools are, after all, intended for single-handed use; forcing a second hand into use may change the body's relationship to the work, affect balance, or even create line-of-sight issues. Instead, when the non-dominant hand isn't needed for the actual task set a firm rule that it should be kept in a specific place. This is easy to do by giving kids a physical reminder of the boundaries, like setting a clamp a safe distance from the action as shown here. The child can still hold the work and steady their stance, as long as the non-dominant hand stays behind the clamp.

All hands on deck

Sometimes the best place for the non-dominant hand to be is in the action. Using a handsaw is a perfect example of a one-handed task, but showing kids how to place a free hand on the work or worksurface – but away from the blade – helps maintain balance and allows them a bit more power in their sawing arm. This young man's left hand isn't actually helping to make the cut since everything (including the miter box) is clamped securely to the worksurface. But in a safe spot behind the clamp, that hand helps balance his stance, with a body posture that keeps him grounded in the task. Plus, it enables you to clearly see both hands at all times while he's working, which is another good safety practice.

Utility screws like these black drywall screws have extremely sharp tips. Instead of digging screws out of their container and risking cut fingers, pour some onto the workbench.

Kids may find a lightweight hammer a better fit for their small hands, instead of the full-size hammer I typically use.

bad enough, but it's now a common practice to apply multiple staples to wood edges that bridge boards to keep them from sliding as they're stacked and shipped. The problem is that once the boards have been separated one end of the staple comes out, resulting in dozens of sharp staple prongs sticking out of board edges, ready to tear skin. Be on the lookout for these when lumber shopping, and remove them immediately with pliers before working the lumber.

Similarly, you expect screws to have sharp tips, but you may not realize just how sharp. Those common black utility or drywall screws are especially sharp, and sometimes have thin spines left from the manufacturing process. These needle-like shards of metal easily break off into fingertips if you're not careful – don't ask me how I know this – so never dig around in a container of screws with your fingers. Instead, pour a few screws onto your worksurface or into a flat tray and pick them up from there.

If you're not sure... Stop!

One of the most common causes of workshop and do-it-yourself accidents is doing something you're not comfortable with. As an adult with decades of woodworking experience, I still firmly believe that if at any time I feel uneasy with a task, I just don't do it. Instead, I'll find some other way with which I'm more comfortable for doing the same thing. This is especially important to remember with children who, by nature, don't have much experience with anything. You know your child, you can read their moods, and you know when they're hesitant to do something in other aspects of their

lives. If you sense hesitance regarding tool use or some other do-it-yourself process, it's time for you to step in and take care of that one yourself. The learning process is a lengthy one and there's plenty of time, so don't let kids do anything they're not sure of.

Likewise, keep a close watch on how they're working, with an eye toward short attention spans. Are they getting tired? Time to stop. Is their concentration wandering? Put things away and come back later. Are they beginning to talk about other things going on in their lives instead of focusing on the task at hand? Put the tools away for the day and pick them back up another time. Children should never perform do-it-yourself work when tired, distracted or in any other way unable to devote 100% attention to what they're doing.

And – I shouldn't have to say it – the same goes for you.

Tools

All the projects that follow can be built with basic tools and materials, so let's take a look at what you'll need. If you have a fully stocked shop with the latest equipment, there's no reason you can't use some of it if you'll take care of some portions of the projects yourself, but I've chosen the following tools for their ease-of-use in small hands.

Hand tools

Basic hand tools form the foundation of what you'll need, beginning with a hammer. I have several in my shop, but

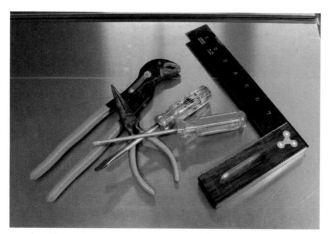

A general assortment of hand tools will come in handy for many do-it-yourself woodworking projects. Shown are regular slip-joint pliers, needle-nose pliers, a square, and both Phillips and flat screwdrivers.

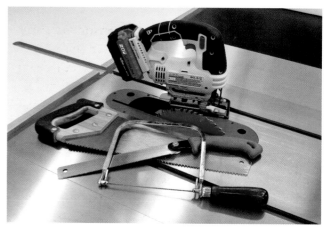

A table saw is fine if you'll do cutting chores yourself, but kids should stick with handsaws or a powered jigsaw for most cuts. Four good choices are (from bottom) a coping saw, Japanese-style pull-saw, a regular handsaw and a cordless jigsaw.

I really only use two of them. For heavy work a regular 16 oz. hammer is a shop staple, but those can be difficult for kids to handle. A smaller hammer – 8 oz. or 10 oz. – is a must for them, plus you may find you also like the little one. A small hammer is perfect for small nails, escutcheon pins, or simply tapping something lightly into place.

Round out your cache of miscellaneous hand tools with at least two screwdrivers, one flat and one Phillips. A variety of sizes of each are good to have to handle the widest range of screws. Speaking of multiples, a couple pairs of pliers will earn their keep in your toolbox. The first type you should have is a pair of adjustable pliers, good for grasping nuts and bolts of any size. As a counterpart, a pair of needle-nose pliers can securely hold a lot of small things.

A good square is a must for drawing 90° cut lines squarely from lumber edges. A combination square that can be adjusted to both 90° and 45° settings is a plus. Squares come in every size imaginable, but if you have only one it should be at least 12" in length. Speaking of measuring, be sure to have a tape measure, yardstick and ruler close at hand. Likewise, a protractor is a useful accessory for laying out angles.

Chisels, scrapers and putty knives come in handy for truing edges or scraping dried glue off projects and worksurfaces. Even a household butter knife can help in a pinch.

Other hand tools to consider include adjustable wrenches, an awl for scoring and marking, a utility knife, and ordinary scissors. A sanding block and an assortment of sandpaper will come into play in almost all the projects. Have #60-grit paper for smoothing extremely rough material, #100-grit for general smoothing and #150-grit for finish work. If you want an even smoother wood surface, having a few sheets of #180- or even #220-grit is a good idea. Finally, a good straightedge is a must, as are pencils. Lots and lots of pencils.

Cutting tools

Every one of the projects in this book is made of wood, which means that one of the most frequent tasks you and your kid will perform is cutting wood. If you have a shop full of machines it's fine to use them if you're doing the cutting, but best to keep the kids away from powerful machines like the table saw. All of the projects can be made with the handsaws.

Handsaws come in a number of types, but among the most useful is a regular, toolbox-length handsaw. These cut on the push stroke and can be very aggressive for cutting wood quickly. They can also be difficult to start cleanly, so you may want to consider starting cuts for your young worker until the blade is set in the wood, and letting them finish the cuts. Of course, letting a kid practice on scrap is always a good idea, and you'll find they'll get the hang of it quickly. Some kids might find it easier to use a Japanese-style pull-saw. Pull-saw teeth face backward, so the saw cuts on the pull stroke as the name implies. These saws are generally thinner and have finer teeth, making them easier to start than regular handsaws. Their fine teeth also leave a cleaner cut edge, especially in softwoods like pine. For cutting curves, a coping saw is perfect. It's not very aggressive so the cut is sometimes slow-going, but it'll cut in any direction and can even cut small circles readily. You'll break fewer blades if you mount the blade to cut on the pull stroke.

If you're comfortable with your young do-it-yourselfer using a bit of power for cutting, a jigsaw is a good introduction. A jigsaw will handle a host of cutting chores, with crosscutting stock to length and ripping workpieces to width the most crucial. A jigsaw's thin blade easily cuts curves and holes, and by adjusting the bottom of the jigsaw you can cut angles and bevels like a pro. Jigsaw blades come in several styles – such as fine-cut and aggressive – so have a variety on hand. A jigsaw with an adjustable orbital action is a good feature to look for. This can adjust the saw to cut very aggressively by forcing the blade forward as it goes up and down, which is ideal for cutting large quantities of wood or making long rip cuts in a board. For finer, cleaner cuts this orbital action can be turned off or to its lowest setting. As with the handsaw, the workpiece must be clamped overhanging the bench before tackling it with a jigsaw.

More power to ponder

Let's take a look at a few more kid-friendly power tools.

Drills

Teamed with a good selection of bits (including spade or Forstner bits that excel at drilling large holes), a cordless electric drill can produce accurate results quickly and reliably. Choose a small drill and most kids will have no trouble handling it. While there are about a dozen kinds of drills, two are the most useful to the young woodworker. A standard drill/driver has two settings – a higher speed with low torque for boring holes with drill bits, and a lower speed with higher torque for driving screws and other fasteners. The second type to consider is a cordless battery-powered screwdriver. These resemble drills, but operate at lower speeds and are intended for driving fasteners only. A dedicated electric screwdriver is much lighter than a regular drill, so it's a lot easier on little arms if they have to drive a lot of screws.

Drill bits are available in a huge range of styles and types, each excelling at a particular task. The four most useful for the projects in this book include a regular twist drill, which is a good all-purpose drill bit for small holes in most materials including metal and plastic. A variation on the twist drill is the brad-point bit, which has a sharp point on the tip that prevents it from wandering or

Kid-friendly power tools include (clockwise from top) a small scroll saw, sander, rotary tool, dedicated power screwdriver and a drill/driver.

(from left) Regular twist drill, brad-point drill, spade bit and Forstner bit.

skating over the surface of the wood as you start drilling (very helpful to kids just learning). For larger holes you'll want either a spade bit – a flat bit with two cutting edges that aggressively and quickly makes holes – or a Forstner bit that cuts a precise flat-bottomed hole. Spade bits are fast, but can leave holes that are a bit on the rough side, while Forstner bits cut more slowly but very smoothly. When given a choice, I always go for the Forstner bit.

Most drill bits have a straight shank of the same diameter as the cutting portion of the drill, and require that you adjust the drill chuck to accommodate them. However, some drills and nearly all powered screwdrivers have ¼" hex chucks you don't need to adjust. The drills for these have a standard ¼" hex shank just like screwdriver bits, meaning that no matter what the actual

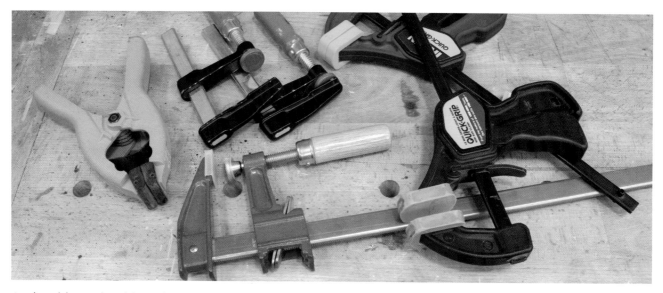

As the old woodworking adage goes, you can't have enough clamps. (clockwise from left) Spring clamp, small F-style bar clamps, one-handed bar clamps, long F-style bar clamp.

drill size the bit will snap into the drill chuck. This is extremely convenient and allows for fast bit changes – say, for example, if you want to go back and forth between drilling pilot holes for screws and driving them in. It's very quick to snap out one and snap in another.

Another advantage of drills with hex-shank ends is that you can slip the bits into extender shafts to lengthen your reach when drilling or driving in hard-to-access places. Depending on the size of the hex chuck on the extender, you can even use them to increase the depth of holes, which will come in handy for the Train Whistle Project in Section Four.

Scroll saw

Scroll saws are benchtop machines that excel at making curved cuts in flat stock, including the most intricate cuts you can imagine. Hence the moniker "scroll" saw – they can scroll. In operation the scroll saw combines the up-and-down action of a jigsaw with a stationary table. Instead of moving the saw through the workpiece, you move the workpiece through the saw. In use, kids can keep their hands plenty far away from the blade. Kids won't be intimidated by the low noise and power rating of most scroll saws, and you'll find that once they get the hang of using one they'll love how it works and the results they can achieve.

Be sure to have an assortment of blades, and read the packaging carefully. You'll find blades rated for aggressive action through thick or hard stock, and delicate

blades for the finest work. The packaging will list the recommended usages.

Sander

We'll use a lot of regular sandpaper and a sanding block in the projects, but you can't beat a power sander for smoothing and finishing larger flat surfaces. The two most common types for one-handed (meaning lightweight) use are the standard orbital sander and the random-orbit sander. The first has a sanding pad that uses a repeating circular motion, while a random-orbit sander's circular motion is just that: random. The advantage is that a random motion doesn't leave swirly patterns on the wood surface, unlike the standard orbital sander. Also, many random-orbit sanders are variable speed, meaning you can cut back on the speed and vibration for light work. Standard orbital sanders are less expensive and can use paper cut from regular sandpaper sheets, while slightly more expensive random-orbit sanders use round sanding discs.

The "select" pine board at the top is clear of knots and other defects, has straight grain and a minimum of cracking and splintering. The regular pine board at the bottom has knots and wild grain. Kids will have an easier time with "select" wood.

Rotary tool

This little jack-of-all-trades is a boon to have in the shop and around the house in general, and you'll find several ways to use one of these tools with the projects. With a spinning motor similar to a drill's, this cylindrical tool is easily operated hand-held and accepts dozens of accessories that turn it into a miniature sander, cutter, polisher, engraver and more. Rotary tools come in several sizes, and in corded and cordless versions. I wouldn't be without one in my shop.

Clamps

In an effort to make projects simple, I've designed several of them to go together with glue only. This saves the step of adding nails or screws for those projects that just don't need the extra strength. Proper glue-ups, though, need to be held securely together until the glue dries. For that, you need clamps. Clamps come in different types and sizes from the literally tiny to several feet in length (I have some five-footers in my shop), but for the projects here the basic ones will do.

Spring clamps are the simplest of the lot, and in operation are really like clothespins – squeeze to open, position on the workpiece, and release to tighten. They're fast and easy to use with only one hand though most kids will need to use two, but most are limited to clamping objects of no more than an inch or two.

Bar clamps are the most useful and versatile for edge-gluing boards together and for assembling projects. One of the jaws ratchets along the length of the bar to approximate the opening needed depending on the size of the workpiece. Once placed on the workpiece the knob is twisted to tighten. Extremely strong, these clamps require both hands to operate. A variant, usually called quick-release clamps, offers single-handed operation. Slide the lower jaw open and set the clamp in place, then close tightly with a pumping action. Light, fast and easy to use, these are the clamps you'll see the most in the project photos.

In addition to clamps that you'll use for glue-ups and actual assembly, be sure to have extras for securing workpieces while building the projects.

Wood

Wood for these projects is pretty basic and I've limited it to only a few types, mostly softwoods like pine and Western red cedar. Both pine and cedar are lightweight, easy to work, inexpensive and readily available at any home center.

Pine is probably the all-around go-to wood for woodworking, and is suitable for almost anything from utility projects to handsome furniture. You'll see a lot of it throughout these pages. Pine comes in a couple of different grades, but I find that "select" pine has few knots, is typically straighter and with few defects, less prone to splitting when nailed and screwed, and generally stronger. Select pine is a bit pricier than No. 2 common, but you'll find it's well worth it for most projects.

Cedar is perfect for projects like the Bird Feeder and Nesting Shelf that will be outside in the weather all the time. Not only does it resist rot and other weather-related damage, but also most insects will leave it alone. And few things smell more wonderful when you're working with it!

Kid-friendly woods include (clockwise from bottom left) Western red cedar, pine, oak, exterior-grade plywood, ½" birch plywood, ¾" birch plywood.

LUMBER DIMENSIONS

When it comes to lumber, what it says ain't necessarily so. Standard wood boards from your local home center are sold as "dimensional lumber," and the actual dimensions are smaller than the nominal dimensions.

Standard "1-by" dimension	Actual dimension	Construction lumber dimension	Actual dimension
1x2	¾" x 1-½"	2x2	1-½" x 1-½"
1x3	¾" x 2-½"	2x4	1-½" x 3-½"
1x4	¾" x 3-½"	2x6	1-½" x 5-½"
1x6	¾" x 5-½"	2x8	1-½" x 7-¼"
1x8	¾" x 7-¼"	2x10	1-½" x 9-¼"
1x10	¾" x 9-¼"	2x12	1-½" x 11-¼"
1x12	¾" x 11-¼"	4x4	3-½" x 3-½"

To make things even easier, whenever possible I've designed the projects to use wood in standard widths, meaning that for many of the projects you'll only need to buy wood of that width and cut the individual workpieces to length. For that reason, you'll see a lot of project components that correspond with standard "dimensional lumber" or "construction lumber," meaning 1-by and 2-by boards in most cases. Keep in mind that lumber dimensions don't match their names, though. A 1x6 board, for example, really measures ¾" x 5-½". I've included a guide for what to expect when shopping for wood in the sidebar "Lumber Dimensions."

I've recommended the hardwoods oak and poplar for some of the projects that require a bit of extra strength but those, too, come in the same dimensions as pine and other softwoods. These woods are harder to cut, and you'll certainly want to drill pilot holes before driving in fasteners of any kind. However, their sleek appearance and strength can be worthwhile for projects that will see a lot of use.

Finally, when you need flat sheet material the best choice is plywood, which comes in a variety of different types. Plain plywood isn't very pretty, and frequently has large flaws and patches on the surface; for utility use or for projects that end up being painted, however, you'll find it the least expensive option. Birch plywood is a bit more expensive, but it has a smooth face-veneer of birch hardwood that can be very attractive with a clear finish like varnish or shellac. Similarly, oak-veneer plywood will bring a touch of class to any project you make. The last type is exterior-grade plywood. Exterior ply isn't the best looking of materials, but with a light sanding and a coat of paint it can look just fine, plus it'll stand up to the elements outdoors.

Glue and fasteners

All the projects in this book go together with glue, nails, screws, or a combination. Sometimes glue does a fine job by itself with no other fasteners required, and whenever possible I've kept things simple by using glue alone. Any time more strength is required, however, it's best to combine glue with mechanical fasteners, either nails or screws.

Any good shop glue – typically called "yellow glue" or "white glue" – is fine, but if something is to be used outdoors or otherwise be exposed to damp conditions, be sure to get a water-resistant or waterproof version. Use glue sparingly. There's no need to have glue oozing out all over everything, which must be cleaned up while still wet or it's difficult to remove. You'll notice in nearly every project that uses glue that I have a rag or paper towel handy to wipe up any glue drips or squeeze-out.

When it comes to mechanical fasteners, nails are about as simple as it gets – point 'em in the right direction and pound 'em in. When hammering nails it's best to drive them in until the nail head is still slightly above the surface, and then drive them the rest of the way with a nail set to place the head flush with or just below the surface of the wood. You'll see me using a nail set several times in the projects that follow. Kids will quickly get the hang of nailing if you have them practice in scrap wood. Don't worry about dinging the wood, and start the nails for little kids so they don't whack their nail-holding fingers.

Screws come in a variety of types. Shown here, from left, are standard black utility screws (sometimes called "drywall" screws), bright zinc-coated screws, exterior-grade screws, and zinc-chromate exterior screws.

Regular common nails have wide, flat heads that are always visible on the wood surface. Finish nails have narrow heads that aren't quite as noticeable, plus they can be driven just below the surface with a nail set and the holes filled with wood putty for true invisibility if desired. Both kinds of nails come in two finishes – regular bright nails are plain, shiny steel with no coatings. These are fine for any indoor projects. For outdoor use, always choose galvanized nails that resist rusting.

Screws come in a variety of styles and types, but for our projects any basic screws will do. When choosing screws keep in mind color and appearance if they'll be visible in the finished work, along with their ability to withstand moisture. For everyday work where neither appearance nor weather resistance is an issue, plain black utility screws – often referred to as "drywall" screws – are fine. These are inexpensive, strong and easy to drive with a Phillips screwdriver or a drill/driver fitted with a Phillips bit.

Three common types of coated screws are readily available in any hardware store or home center. These include bright silver zinc-coated screws, an all-around screw with lots of applications and reasonable resistance to damp weather. Coated exterior screws have a finish, usually gray or tan in color, that's often epoxy-based and very weather resistant. Zinc chromate-coated screws are very resistant to moisture and are gaining popularity with woodworkers. I also like them for general use even when the project won't be exposed to the weather, because their soft bronze color blends well with wood, making them less obtrusive in applications where they aren't hidden.

Coatings

There's absolutely nothing wrong with not applying paint or other coating. Any project can be left plain. In fact, some projects – like the Nesting Shelf and Bird Feeder projects – are better left uncoated. Paints or varnishes could be harmful to birds, plus the cedar we'll use for those projects is both attractive and naturally resistant to the elements. However, we will use a finish of some type on several other projects.

Paint is an obvious choice, especially when you want to match a particular color scheme in the home. For example, you'll notice in the Desktop Bookrack Project that I've chosen a soft almond paint that goes well with the wall color and the stained oak of the desk where it'll be used. Stick with acrylic latex paints that dry quickly and are relatively easy to clean up afterward with soap and water. If projects will be used outdoors, like the Cornhole Game, exterior latex paint is the right choice.

When you want the beauty of the grain to show through, especially for oak or other hardwoods, choose a clear finish like polyurethane varnish. Polyurethane dries very hard and offers a lot of protection, plus it gives a warm glow to wood grain. Polyurethane doesn't dry very quickly, so if you're looking for a fast turnaround after coating a project, consider shellac, a traditional clear coating that has been used for generations.

Whether you choose paint, varnish or shellac, you have the choice between buying it in a can and applying it with a brush, or in an aerosol version that sprays on. You'll see both used in the projects here. If you do like the ease of spraying finishes, try spray lacquer. Available in clear and in colors, it's among the fastest-drying wood finishes and comes in both gloss and matte formulations.

Finally, if you just want to bring out the grain and add a bit of color, but don't need the extreme protection of a hard coating like paint or varnish, another option is linseed oil. A traditional finish that's hundreds of years old, linseed oil is easy to apply. Just brush or wipe on a coat of the oil and let it absorb into the wood for 15 or 20 minutes, then wipe of the excess. Allow the project to dry for at least 24 hours then buff the wood surface and you're done. You can easily renew the finish as it wears by just giving it a new coat periodically. Be sure to allow any oily rags to thoroughly air-dry before disposal.

Techniques

I noted at the outset that this book isn't an all-encompassing tutorial on woodworking, but we will use a lot of interesting techniques throughout the projects. Rather than overload this opening chapter I'll save a lot of the specific techniques for when they come up in the projects and describe them there. However, there are some woodworking procedures that are important to most if not all the projects here and woodworking in general. Let's take a look at two you should always have in your arsenal of skills.

Cutting square and straight

Sometimes squareness doesn't matter (in fact, some of the projects are made entirely with curved cuts), but when it does you'll want to ensure that you're cutting as straight and true as possible.

Any time the end of a workpiece must be perfectly square – or cut to a reliable 45° angle – clamp the wood in a miter box to crosscut boards to length.

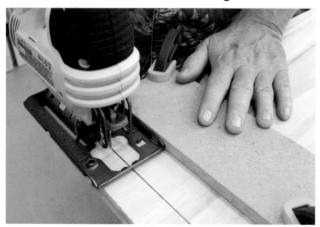

To make perfectly straight cuts with a jigsaw, guide the saw's base against a strip of wood clamped to your workpiece and workbench.

For crosscutting, usually done to cut wood to length, a miter box is the perfect choice. Most miter boxes will accommodate boards up to 5" or 6" in width, and have guide slots for your saw to make 90° and 45° crosscuts, and 45° bevel cuts. I generally just hold the board in place when using a miter box, but I recommend always clamping the board and the miter box securely to a bench or other worksurface for kids, who may not have enough arm strength to keep the workpiece steady.

Using wood in the widths it comes right off the rack means you won't have to do many long rip cuts lengthwise in boards. However, to make straight crosscuts in boards too wide for a miter box, or for long cuts in boards or any lengthy cut in plywood, the photo at the lower left shows a great technique for making perfectly straight cuts with a jigsaw. Use a square and straightedge to mark the cut line on your workpiece. Now, hold your jigsaw against the cut line and place a strip of wood – a length of 1x2 or 1x3 works great – against the base of the jigsaw so it's offset from the cut line by the width of the jigsaw, and clamp it to the workpiece to act as a cutting guide. Pressing the jigsaw against the edge of guide keeps it moving in a perfectly straight line as you make the cut. Not only does this method make it far easier for a child to get great results, the ease of the cut means they can concentrate fully on using the tool as opposed to worrying about how straight the line of cut is.

Pilot holes

There's always a danger of splitting wood when driving nails or screws, especially with the soft pine we'll use for many of the projects. Even when splitting isn't an issue, driving steel into wood can require a lot of muscle when you've not prepped the wood to receive the fasteners. This is especially problematic for kids, leading to slipped screwdrivers and bent nails. Avoid all these problems by drilling a pilot hole before driving fasteners into place.

For nails, you can create a proper pilot hole by using one of the nails themselves as a makeshift drill bit. Clip the head of the nail off with a pair of angled pliers, as shown in the photo on page 17. Now, chuck the headless nail into your drill or drill/driver, and bore a pilot hole into the first of the two pieces of wood you'll be nailing together. With softwoods like pine and cedar it's often only necessary to drill the top piece; when you nail it into

A great tip for making nails easier to drive is to use one as a pilot "drill bit." Clip off the nail head with angled pliers, then use the clipped nail to bore a pilot hole in the workpieces.

place the pilot hole guides the nail solidly into the second piece. For hardwoods, though, it's best to clamp the two workpieces together and drill both at the same time.

Do the same thing for screws, but instead you'll use a regular drill bit sized to match the shank of the screw; that is, the solid portion of the screw inside the threads.

To keep screws less obtrusive, always countersink the pilot holes when you drill them so the screws will rest flush with the surface of the wood or slightly below it. Countersink bits come in two types. The first is used to create a funnel-shaped depression right over the pilot hole you've already drilled. The other type drills the pilot hole and countersink at the same time. This is incredibly handy, and the method I prefer.

Normally when countersinking screws you drill just deep enough so the screw will be flush, but if you really want to hide screws drill the countersink about ¼" to ⅜" below the surface, which will leave an open hole above the screw head. Then after you drive it in you can glue in a wooden plug to make the screw vanish. We'll use this technique in the Desktop Bookrack Project, and I'll describe it in detail there.

OK, I think we've covered most of the basics you need to get going, but remember that I'll go over some techniques and procedures in considerably more detail as they come up in the projects. So if you're all ready, grab your tools and grab a kid.

Let's get building!

Two common types of countersink bits. The black one bores both the countersink and pilot hole at the same time; the gold bit bores the countersink after you've already made a pilot hole.

With the workpieces glued and clamped, drill countersunk pilot holes to prepare for driving screws.

Getting Started

Gwen's Toolbox

Every kid needs a toolbox. Whether the tools are their own or borrowed from your shop, a personal toolbox lends a sense of ownership and responsibility for both the tools and the project. On the practical side, kids like toolboxes for the same reasons you do: They make things easier to carry, it keeps them organized while working, and it makes straightening up much easier.

To accomplish this first project in the book, I got some help from Gwen, my wife's cousin's granddaughter. I think that makes her my first cousin twice removed, but I'm not sure how genealogy works on that. One thing I am sure of is that Gwen, like all kids, was eager to jump right in and get started. Even more so when I told her the toolbox was hers to keep when we were done. Her

comment on learning this was, "I guess I better do a real good job, then, huh?"

This particular toolbox design is probably hundreds of years old, and you can see them in the oldest photography. That's because it's simple to make and even easier to customize, which I'll describe at the end of the project. The basic design consists of a pair of ends shaped to hold an elevated handle, a sturdy dowel handle sandwiched between the two ends, and three rectangular pieces for the lower container. You can use any kind of wood for the project – really heavy-duty versions are often made of hardwood – but let's stick with light, easy-to-work pine.

Gwen's Toolbox

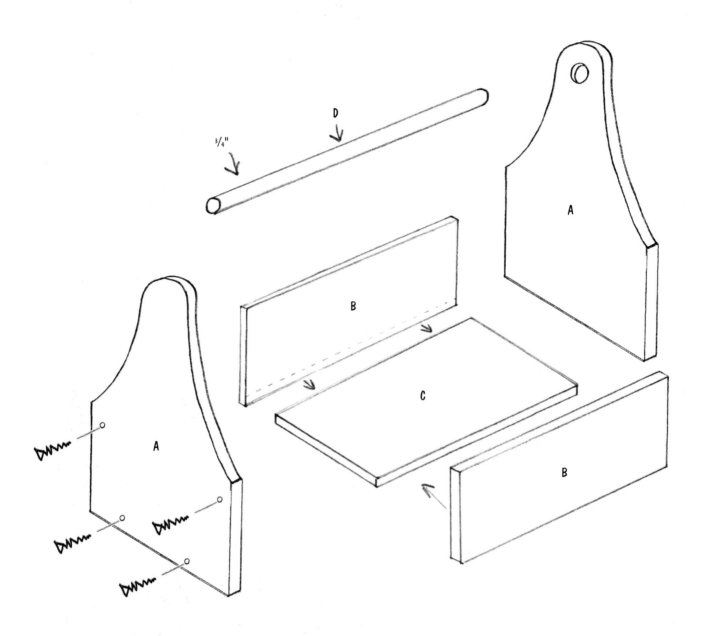

Gwen's Toolbox Cut List

Overall dimensions: 13-½" long x 7-¼" wide x 10" tall

Ref	Qty.	Part	Stock	Thick	Width	Length
A	2	Ends	Pine	¾"	7-¼"	10"
B	2	Sides	Pine	¾"	3-½"	12"
C	1	Bottom	Pine	¾"	5-½"	12"
D	1	Handle	Poplar	¾"	n/a	13"

Building the Toolbox

Begin by cutting the flat stock to size. As we work through the projects that follow we'll use a number of methods to cut project components, but we'll start out here with a basic handsaw. Like most of the projects in this book, the toolbox uses off-the-shelf 1-by lumber, which eliminates the need to cut wood to width. This introductory project uses standard 1x8 boards for the toolbox ends, 1x6 lumber for the bottom and 1x4 lumber for the sides, which means we'll only have to cut parts to length. Remember, though, that the actual widths are 7-¼", 5-½" and 3-½", respectively.

To get a square cut with a handsaw you can't beat a miter box, which you can see in Photo 1. Most adults are fine using a miter box by just holding it and the workpiece by hand, but note here that I've securely clamped both the stock and the miter box to the worktable to make things easier for Gwen. This is always a good idea for kids, who may not be physically strong enough nor well enough coordinated to hold everything, and instead allows them to concentrate on safely making the cut.

With the five flat pieces cut to length, let's sand the bottom and side pieces and glue up the lower container. This is a simple process of just gluing the sides to the edges of the bottom, making sure the three pieces are perfectly aligned at both ends, and then clamping the three pieces together until the glue dries (Photo 2). These edge-to-face joints are long-grain glue joints and so are extremely strong; you don't need any additional fasteners for a light-duty toolbox like this.

While the container is drying, trace the pattern from page 22 (also available for download at PopularWoodworking.com/HamlerBook) onto the end workpieces. To accurately locate the hole for the handle, use an awl to mark its center right through the pattern, as in Photo 3. The dimple left by the awl not only marks the location of the hole center, but also acts as a starting point for the drill bit.

You can make the curved cuts like those on the end pieces a number of ways, but for the projects in this book we'll stick with coping saw, jigsaw, or scroll saw. I've found that when it comes to kid-friendly power equipment, the scroll saw is a winner. It's an inexpensive machine, relatively quiet in use, and it easily cuts intricate curves and designs. Most important, the cutting action is slow – the scroll saw doesn't zip through a piece of wood with a table saw's laser speed – making it a safer option power-wise, plus when used properly little hands

Photo 1 To make it easier for kids to saw, securely clamp the miter box and workpiece to a sturdy worksurface.

Photo 2 Edge-to-face glue joints are plenty strong in this application without additional fasteners. Be sure that the ends of all three pieces line up flush.

Photo 3 Marking hole locations with an awl gives the drill bit a positive start for drilling.

Toolbox End Pattern

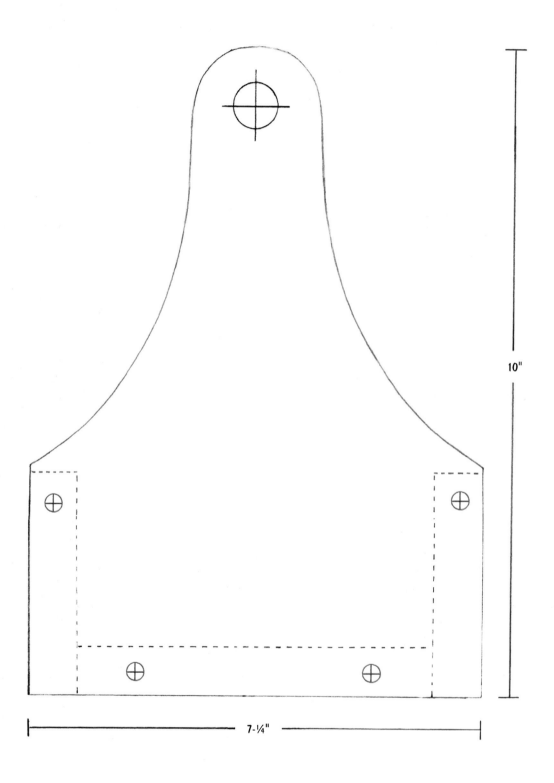

10"

7-¼"

are plenty far away from the blade. You'll see all three of these sawing methods used throughout the projects, but for this lead project let's stick with the scroll saw.

Gwen wasn't the least bit intimidated by the scroll saw (it's quiet, not scary-loud), but all the same I made sure to be very close until she got used to how it worked (Photo 4). Standing directly behind her also gave me a good viewing angle to see that she was following the cut line, and to give guidance as needed.

Now, if you have one in your shop and prefer to do the cutting yourself for your little woodworker, a band saw will make quick work of any curved cut. However, I wouldn't recommend it for kid use.

The holes for the ¾" dowel handle must be drilled to a precise depth and perfectly straight, so you might want to handle this task. The holes don't go all the way through the end pieces, just ½" deep. In Photo 5, with the workpiece clamped to my bench I'm using a ¾" Forstner bit to drill the hole. The business end of the drill happens to be exactly ½" high, so drilling the hole to the precise depth was just a matter of stopping when the back of the cutter was level with the workpiece. If your Forstner bit's cutter is of a different height, or if you're using a spade or other bit, use a piece of masking tape to mark the bit at ½", and stop drilling when you reach the tape.

With all the parts cut, a good sanding is in order before assembly (Photo 6). A sanding block works best for sanding the faces of all the flat pieces. A piece of folded sandpaper works well for the curved edges of the end pieces. A dedicated spindle sander would make quick work of this task if you have one in your shop, as would a small sanding drum on a rotary tool – a technique we'll use in later projects.

At this point you're nearly ready to assemble the toolbox, but before you grab glue and screws, do a quick dry assembly just to check how everything fits. You should always do a dry fit of project parts before you commit to permanent fasteners and glue. If there are any issues with fit or parts that aren't quite right, you want to know that, and fix it, before adding any glue.

Photo 4 Start slowly when introducing youngsters to power tools, and stay close for both guidance and security.

Photo 5 Forstner bits are perfect for drilling stopped holes in the toolbox ends.

Photo 6 Sanding before assembly is always easier and more efficient.

As you do the dry assembly, you'll notice that the lower container subassembly is slightly narrower than the two ends. This is perfectly fine, and owes to the fact that we're using standard dimensional lumber. The ends, cut from 1x8, measure 7-¼". The box bottom, cut from 1x6, measures 5-½". When the lower container is assembled, the total width after adding the two ¾"-thick sides is exactly 7". This extra width results in about ⅛" on each side when the lower container is centered on the end piece.

For the final assembly, apply glue to the ends of the lower container and place it in position on the inside of one of the end pieces, then insert the dowel handle into its hole as shown in Photo 7. Apply glue to the remaining end of the lower container and put the other end piece into place, taking care to seat the handle dowel in its hole.

Shift the assembly so it rests flat on your worksurface, and clamp the parts together. Unlike the naturally strong long-grain joints of the box sides, attaching the ends creates an end-grain to face-grain joint – also called a butt joint – so you'll need the extra strength that screws bring to the party. Drill countersunk pilot holes as described on pages 16-17, then drive four 1-½" to 1-¾" screws as indicated on the End Pattern drawing on page 22 (Photo 8). Depending on how you clamped up the assembly, you may need to drill only two pilot holes at a time on each end and drive the corresponding screws, then reset the clamps to drill and drive the remaining two screws.

With the screws set and the glue dry, remove the clamps and the toolbox is done – almost. Your budding woodworker is going to be extremely proud of the finished toolbox, so make it complete by both of you signing it somewhere. (This isn't just a kid thing by the way: I've been signing everything I make for decades!) In Photo 9, you can see that Gwen and I have both signed the bottom of the toolbox, plus she's decided to add some decoration of her own to fully personalize it.

Photo 7 It's essential to have everything close at hand – glue, fasteners, drill/driver, clamps – during assembly.

Photo 8 Even for tasks a child might not be quite strong enough to handle, they can still be actively involved in project steps that you tackle.

Photo 9 Personalizing projects with signatures is a touch that will last for years.

Once the work is signed, you can begin using the toolbox immediately. Or, if you prefer, you can add the finish of your choice. A few coats of clear polyurethane will help to bring out the wood's grain, plus it'll add a measure of protection. Painting it any bright color might be a lot of fun, too, but it's just fine if you want to leave the wood plain.

This is a good project to customize. The most obvious choice is to change the dimensions of the parts for a different size toolbox, but keep in mind the limits of how much weight the child will be carrying. A larger toolbox may be only slightly heavier – pine is pretty light, after all – but a larger capacity means that more tools could quickly weigh the box down.

Dividers can be useful, so consider dividing the interior of the container lengthwise, leaving one side as-is for longer tools, and perhaps subdividing the other to organize smaller items like screws and nails.

To make it more versatile, consider drilling a few vertical holes in the top edges of the box sides to accommodate screwdrivers, pencils or other slim items. This will keep the main box open for larger tools, and prevent smaller things from cluttering up the interior and getting lost there.

Finally, a project of this type doesn't really have to be relegated to woodworking and do-it-yourself tasks. Instead of using it as a toolbox, it can become any kind of tote your child wants it to be.

GOING WITH THE GRAIN

When joining wood, particularly with glue alone, how one surface meets another determines how strong the joint is. The terminology for these joints is based on the grain direction of the workpieces.

Long-grain to long-grain joints are those where the grain runs in the same direction. This can include wood joined edge-to-edge, face-to-face and edge-to-face. Most long-grain glue joints are straight, not angled, and are among the strongest you can create. In fact, the glue joint is often stronger than the wood itself.

End-grain to long-grain describes joints that are typically angled, where the end of one workpiece is glued to the face or long edge of another. Also called "butt joints." When made with glue alone this joint isn't noted for strength and is suited for light-duty use only. For best results, before assembling the joint size the end grain component with a dilute coat of glue and let it dry. To make a really strong butt joint, add nails, screws, or other fasteners.

End-grain to end-grain joints are the weakest of glue joints, and are not suited to uses under weight. For very small workpieces that don't receive much stress or sideways movement, however, these joints can be acceptable.

Frank's Workbench

Now that we have a toolbox, the next essential for young woodworkers is some place to work wood. Any table or workbench you already have will do in a pinch, but most kids aren't tall enough to work comfortably at one of those without standing on something. That'll do if you have no choice, but wouldn't their own workbench sized just for them be a lot better? My friend Frank, who lives a few houses down from us, definitely agreed with that

idea so I invited him over for the afternoon to build him a personalized workbench.

Like the toolbox, we'll use off-the-shelf lumber, in this case select pine 1x2 and 1x3 boards. (Which, remember, are really 1-½" and 2-½" wide, respectively.) For the benchtop I chose a sheet of ½" birch plywood, which will keep the overall weight down yet still be strong enough for a workbench of this size.

Photo 1 A good height for a workbench is the distance from floor to wrist.

Photo 2 Whenever possible, clamp workpieces securely before cutting to make the task easier and safer.

Photo 3 A glue brush helps to keep small hands clean. But have a rag or paper towel handy.

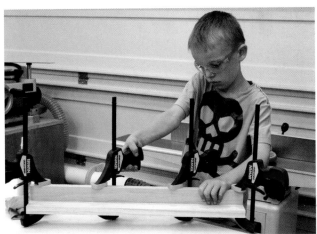

Photo 4 Assembling the leg components in an "L" shape makes for a sturdy workbench.

The width and length of the bench will be 18-½" x 30", a good working space for most kid-sized projects, but we'll set the height to exactly fit Frank's needs. A good rule of thumb for workbench height is that it should come up to about wrist level, so I had Frank stand up straight and held a yardstick next to him so that one end is on the floor and the stick rested against his arm as in Photo 1. I got a measurement of 23-½", about what I expected for a seven-year-old boy, so that's the total height the bench will be. Subtracting the thickness of the plywood benchtop from that height gives a length of 23" for the legs.

One thing to keep in mind is the fact that your child will likely outgrow it pretty soon. For that reason, when measuring and deciding on a height always err on the high side. They'll soon grow into a workbench that's just a bit too high, but working at a too-low bench quickly becomes uncomfortable.

Building the Workbench

Each of the four legs is made up of a piece of 1x2 and 1x3 joined in an "L" shape. To begin, cut four pieces of each width wood to 23" in length, by the method of your choice. You'll see a variety of cutting methods throughout this book, but here we'll use a jigsaw. Whenever kids are cutting wood you should firmly clamp it to a steady support, and in Photo 2 you can see that I've clamped the wood to a small sawhorse.

Assemble the legs by first applying glue to one edge of a 1x2 workpiece (Photo 3). Now, if it were just me and the camera wasn't around I'd probably just spread the glue with a fingertip, but as you can see I'm instilling good habits in my young assistant by having him use a brush.

To create the "L" shape, place the glued edge of the 1x2 onto the face of a 1x3 workpiece flush against one side, then clamp up as in Photo 4. Set the assembly aside to dry and repeat the process for the other three legs.

Frank's Workbench

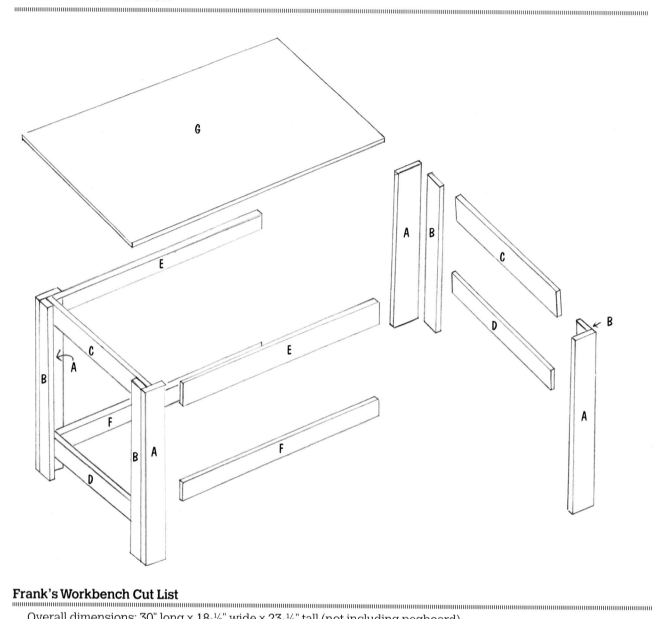

Frank's Workbench Cut List

Overall dimensions: 30" long x 18-½" wide x 23-½" tall (not including pegboard)

Ref	Qty.	Part	Stock	Thick	Width	Length
A	4	Leg, Wide Sides	Pine	¾"	2-½"	23"
B	4	Leg, Narrow Sides	Pine	¾"	1-½"	23"
C	2	Upper End Stretchers	Pine	¾"	2-½"	15-½"
D	2	Lower End Stretchers	Pine	¾"	1-½"	15-½"
E	2	Upper Front/Back Stretcher	Pine	¾"	2-½"	24"
F	2	Lower Front/Back Stretcher	Pine	¾"	1-½"	24"
G	1	Worktop	Plywood	½"	18-½"	30"

Notes

Parts A through F are standard select pine lumber with nominal dimensions of 1x2 and 1x3.

Additional Hardware

1" x 1" steel brackets (6 needed)

When the glue has dried and you've unclamped the legs, if you take a close look at them you'll see that one side of the "L" shape is ¼" longer than the other. This is due to the size of the standard 1-by lumber we used, which makes one side of the leg 2-½", and the other 2-¼". This isn't an issue at all, but you do need to keep this size difference in mind in the next step.

We'll assemble the legs in pairs to create sets, connect the sets with stretchers, and then add the benchtop at the end of the project. Making a leg set is straightforward, and we'll start with the ends by arranging two legs on a worksurface. It doesn't matter which way you orient the legs – wide-side down, or narrow-side down – because it doesn't affect the assembly process. However, for the sake of appearance you'll want to orient everything the same direction. I decided to arrange the legs so that in the finished workbench the wider sides of the legs face forward and back, with the narrow portions facing to the sides.

Assemble the leg sets by attaching one upper end stretcher (Part C on the Cut List) between the legs flush at the top, and a lower end stretcher (Part D) between the legs at about 4" from the bottom. Apply glue to the mating surfaces and hold the assembly together with clamps. Now, drill a pair of countersunk pilot holes in the ends of the top stretcher and a single pilot hole in the ends of the lower one, and drive in 1-¼" screws to secure the legs (Photo 5). With the screws in place you can remove the clamps, then repeat the process to create the other leg set.

With the end leg sets complete, connect them with the upper and lower front/back stretchers (Parts E and F) in the same manner. The resulting four-legged assembly will make the perfect base for the workbench.

Making the benchtop is just a simple process of cutting it to size from a larger sheet of plywood. We'll use the jigsaw with an appropriate blade and we'll set up the saw for a good-quality cut. The veneer on plywood can be fragile, and cutting often splinters the surface veneer, called "tear-out." To avoid this, choose a blade rated for plywood, with a high tooth count and a tooth grind that's kind to veneers. These come with names like "clean-cut" or "fine-cut" or something similar, and often list their appropriateness for plywood on the package.

In addition to a proper blade, pay attention to the saw's cut characteristics. Many jigsaws have a control setting for what's called "orbital action." In additional to going up and down, an aggressive orbital action pushes the blade forward and slightly into the wood on the up-stroke. This

Photo 5 Starting with the workbench ends, attach the upper and lower stretchers with glue and countersunk screws.

Photo 6 A clamped-on guide helps make perfectly straight cuts in the plywood workbench top.

Photo 7 Center the up-ended leg set on the underside of the benchtop.

Photo 8 Simple metal brackets secure the leg set from underneath the plywood top. Be sure to use short screws that won't go all the way through the plywood.

Photo 9 A final once-over with a sanding block will smooth any sharp edges.

makes for a powerful cut that's great for blasting through solid wood or for rough construction chores, but it's not what you want for plywood. So if your jigsaw has this feature, choose its lowest setting for the cleanest cut.

To make the plywood cuts as straight as possible, prepare a simple cutting guide as described in the opening section (page 16). In Photo 6, you can see that I've clamped a piece of regular 1x2 to the plywood so that the jigsaw's blade aligns with the cut lines Frank and I drew on the workpiece. As you push the saw forward through the cut, make sure that the side of its base plate hugs that wooden guide strip, and you'll get a perfectly straight line. We'll use this technique a number of times throughout the book, and it's a great one to teach to new woodworkers.

To mount the benchtop, set it upside down on a worktable or sawhorse as in Photo 7, then upend the assembled leg set and center it on the top. Secure 1" x 1" steel brackets to the stretchers – two evenly spaced on the front and back, and one centered on each end – with screws. When the brackets are mounted on the stretchers, secure them to the underside of the benchtop with ½" screws (Photo 8). Even though the top is only ½" thick, the brackets are thick enough to keep the screws from going all the way through the wood.

With the workbench now fully assembled, give it a good sanding all around to remove rough or sharp edges as in Photo 9. At this point, the workbench is ready to receive a few coats of polyurethane varnish, or you can put it right to use.

SHELF IMPROVEMENT

Want to make this basic workbench even more versatile? That's easy to do by adding a utility shelf underneath for storing a toolbox, clamps, or small power tools. The best part is that the design of the lower stretchers makes the workbench ready to customize.

Those lower stretchers make a perfect ledge for a shelf. Guided by the stretcher lengths, cut a piece of ½" plywood to 15-½" x 25-½". Sand the edges of the plywood thoroughly all around.

Tilt the plywood between the legs and slip it into place, allowing it to rest on the stretchers. You can attach the shelf to the stretchers with a few 1" screws if you like, but it's not necessary. The shelf is neatly trapped inside the structure and anything stored there will weigh it down securely.

Since Frank is likely to outgrow his bench pretty fast, we added some extenders to the legs like the one in Photo 10. This is merely a piece of 1x2 cut to fit beneath where the lower stretchers meet in the inside corners. Here, I've taken a 4" length of 1x2 and drilled ¼" holes 1" apart, plus a single hole through the leg 1" from the bottom. Slip a bolt through the hole from the outside of the leg and into the lowest hole in the extender, and secure it with a washer and wing nut. When the bench becomes a little low for easy use just slip out the bolt, relocate it into the next higher hole, and replace the wing nut. Bingo, the workbench is now an inch higher. The extender shown will gain you a couple extra inches, and after that you can make longer extenders.

Better yet, it might just be time to make a brand-new workbench together, custom-sized for your growing woodworker.

Photo 10 Plan for the future with leg extenders to raise the workbench height as your little woodworker grows.

Pegboard Tool Rack

For the final of our three introductory projects, let's make something that complements both of the previous ones. As an accessory to the workbench, this tool rack keeps everything out right in front of the work area within easy reach. A sheet of pegboard and a handful of assorted pegboard hooks will do the trick.

Building the Tool Rack

For cutting the pegboard, arrange the sheet on a worksurface with the "good" side that will be the front – the smoothest side – down. Jigsaws cut on the upstroke, and the extremely soft material tends to be rough on the upper side no matter how you set the saw's orbital action, so you'll want any roughness to be on the back. You can

Pegboard Tool Rack

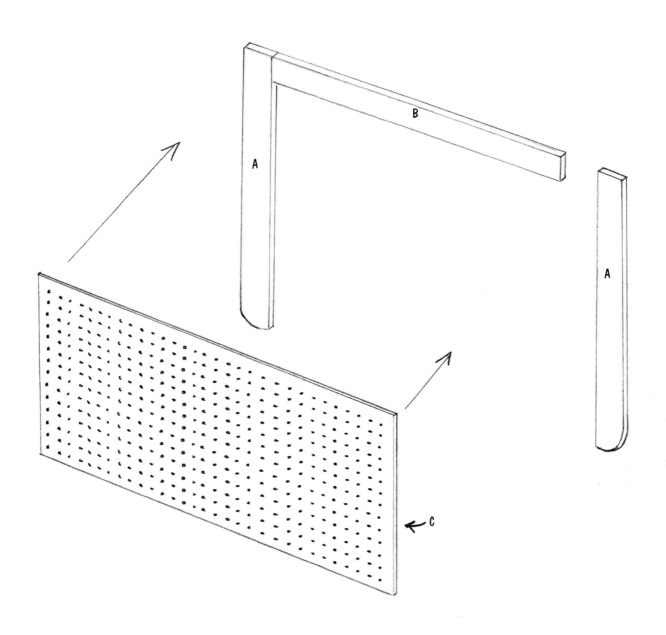

Pegboard Tool Rack Cut List

Overall dimensions: 30" long x 1" thick x 21" tall (not including lower mounting portion)

Ref	Qty.	Part	Stock	Thick	Width	Length
A	2	Frame Sides	Pine	¾"	2-½"	27"
B	1	Frame Top Stretcher	Pine	¾"	1-½"	25"
C	1	Rack	Pegboard	¼"	21"	30"

Note
Parts A and B are standard 1x3 and 1x2 lumber.

Additional Hardware
Pegboard hooks in various sizes and configurations

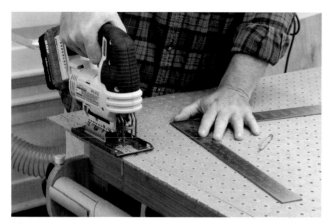

Photo 1 When cutting pegboard, sometimes it's just a matter of connecting the dots.

Photo 2 Cutting pegboard can leave a rough edge, but a small plane or a sanding block will smooth the soft material quickly.

Photo 3 Cut the curve at the bottom of the frame sides with a jigsaw.

Photo 4 Pegboard glues very securely to bare wood, so no other fasteners are required. The brick is being used to clamp one of the frame pieces.

clamp a temporary guide strip of 1x2 to the workpiece if you like, but pegboard is very easy to cut, so I've chosen to just cut freehand in Photo 1. Simply eyeballing the pattern of holes acts as a visual guide.

Smooth the cut edges with a sanding block or small plane (Photo 2). As with cutting, the soft material cleans up very easily and quickly.

Cut the frame pieces to length from standard 1x3 for the sides and 1x2 for the top stretcher. The stretcher ends will butt up against the frame sides, so ensure squareness on the ends by using a miter box and handsaw to make the cuts.

The final step of stock preparation is to round off one bottom corner of each frame side piece, as in Photo 3. I've used a jigsaw here, but a scroll saw would also handle the task. The tool rack will exactly match the length of the workbench top from the previous project, but remember that the benchtop overhangs the leg set a bit. By putting a curve on the outside edges of the frame

sides it'll help to create a smooth transition, as you'll see shortly. The exact size of the rounded curve isn't critical at all, so trace around any round object you have handy (I used a soda can).

To assemble the tool rack, do a dry-fit of the components on the back side of the pegboard and use a pencil to trace the inside edge of each component. Now, apply a bit of glue inside your pencil marks; the fibrous nature of pegboard, especially on the rough back side, adheres very well to wood so you won't need a lot. In Photo 4, you can see how I basically just applied the glue in a grid pattern down the length of the sheet, avoiding the peg holes. Drop the frame pieces into the pencil outlines and press them into place. At this point you can clamp them in place, but it's really just as easy to weight them down till the glue dries with whatever heavy objects you have at hand – paint can, heavy book or a brick as I've done here.

Photo 5 With the completed rack clamped to the workbench, drill countersunk pilot holes and screw it securely in place.

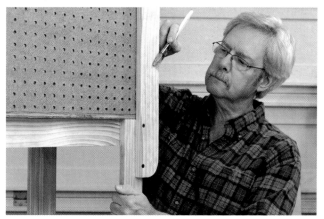

Photo 6 You can leave the rack's wood frame plain, or give it a few protective coats of polyurethane varnish.

This is a very small pegboard rack and tools on it won't weigh much, so there's really no need to do more than butt the side pieces and the top stretcher together with a bit of glue at the corners. The pegboard itself will hold the frame rigid, so no additional fasteners are needed to join the frame pieces.

When everything is dry, place the rack onto the rear edge of the workbench and clamp the lower portion of the side pieces to the rear workbench legs, then drill a pair of countersunk pilot holes through the back and into both rear legs, as in Photo 5. Drive 1-¼" screws into the pilot holes to secure the rack to the workbench. Don't use any glue for this, by the way. You may want to remove the pegboard rack to transport the workbench, and just removing the screws will allow you to take it off quickly.

Finally, since I gave the workbench from the previous project several coats of polyurethane varnish, I decided to do the same with the wooden components of the rack (Photo 6).

You can find pegboard hooks at any hardware store or home center in a variety of styles. In addition to simple hooks, some are shaped for specific uses like holding hammers, screwdrivers, and other tools. How you arrange them is limited only by your imagination.

Or, more accurately, your kid's.

Games

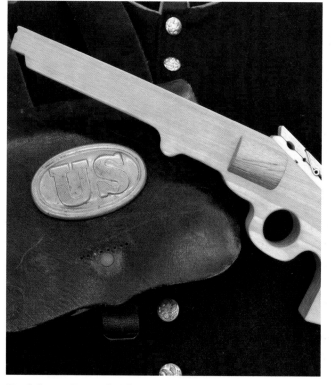

Cornhole Game

Target games have been popular for millennia. Some have evolved into professional sports like soccer, basketball and hockey, but most were embraced by the public at large for their own leisure activities. It's a rare backyard that hasn't seen a target competition among excited groups of kids (and adults, too).

One particular target game that has grown in popularity in recent years is based on the old beanbag carnival games. It's known by several names – tailgate, corn toss, bags, baggo and simply bag toss to name a few – but you probably know it as cornhole. The game consists of a playing board measuring 24" x 48", with a 6" hole near the top. Legs or other supports raise the back of the board to a height of 12" to tilt it toward the players, who attempt to throw bags of dried corn through the hole. It couldn't be simpler.

Simple or not, the game is so popular that a number of organizations have sprung up for enthusiasts, with the similarly named American Cornhole Association and the American Cornhole Organization being the two largest and best known. These groups are a wellspring of information on the game, including official rules, regional competitions, playing tips, and the like. The rules for the game, as well as the specifications for the game board, are nearly the same for the two groups.

There's a lot of wood in this project, so I've designed it to keep both material cost and overall weight to a minimum. As with most projects in this book the cornhole board can be made with off-the-shelf plywood and standard 1-by pine.

Cornhole Game

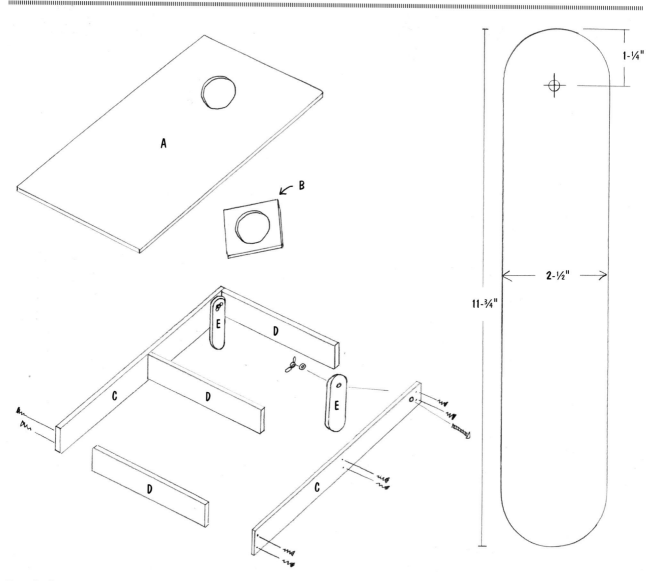

Cornhole Game Cut List

Overall dimensions: 24" wide x 48" deep x 12" high (with legs in open position)

Ref	Qty.	Part	Stock	Thick	Width	Length
A	1	Top	Plywood	¼"	24"	48"
B	1	Hole Reinforcement	Plywood	¼"	8"	8"
C	2	Frame Sides	Pine	¾"	2-½"	48" (a)
D	3	Frame Ends/Middle	Pine	¾"	2-½"	22-½" (a)
E	2	Legs	Pine	¾"	2-½"	11-¾" (a)

Additional Hardware

2" carriage bolts (2 needed)

¼" washers (2 needed)

¼" wing nuts (2 needed)

Notes

(a) Parts C, D, and E are standard 1x3 pine, which actually measures ¾" thick by 2-½" wide.

Photo 1 A compass and ruled guidelines help to accurately place the hole reinforcement.

Photo 2 Spread glue on the back of the plywood hole reinforcement.

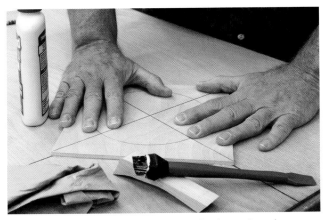

Photo 3 Match the guidelines on the board to those on the back of the reinforcement.

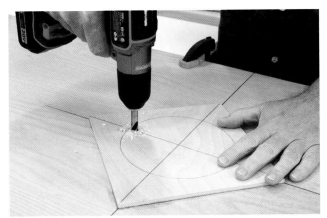

Photo 4 Drill a ½" pilot hole as a starting point for cutting.

Building the Cornhole Game

We'll start construction with the game surface, which is ¼" plywood. Hardwood veneer plywood is best, as it offers the smoothest surface and is more attractive if you decide to finish it with a clear varnish instead of paint. I used oak veneer plywood since it's what I had on hand, but birch ply would work just as well. Whichever type you use, you'll find it available in 24" x 48" sheets at any home center so you won't need to cut it to size.

Prepare this plywood by drawing guidelines to locate the hole on what will be the underside of the game surface. We'll use a jigsaw to cut the target hole, and since jigsaws can splinter a bit on the upper surface of the workpiece we'll do all our layout and cutting from the underside.

First, draw a line across the width of the plywood 9" below the top edge, followed by a second line perpendicular to the first and exactly centered on the sheet. No need to draw this second line all the way to the bottom, but it should cross the first line and extend about 7" below it. The intersection of the two lines locates the center of the 6" target hole.

Because we're using ¼" plywood, let's reinforce the target hole. Cut an 8" x 8" square of ¼" plywood and draw lines corner-to-corner to locate the center. Set a compass for a 3" radius, and draw a 6" circle on workpiece as in Photo 1.

Flip the piece over and spread glue evenly over the back. In Photo 2 I'm using a glue brush, but you could also use a piece of cardboard or an old playing card (or even a credit card!) to spread the glue.

Now, press it into place glue-side down so all the guidelines line up, as in Photo 3. You won't be able to clamp this piece, so hold it in place with some heavy objects till the glue dries. A few bricks or gallon paint cans will do the trick.

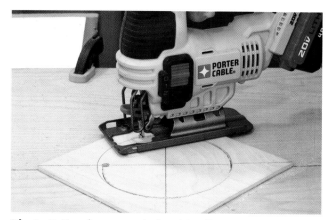

Photo 5 Cut the target hole with a jigsaw.

Photo 6 Sand away any splintering and roughness from the freshly cut edges of the target hole.

Photo 7 Lay out the location for the middle frame piece at 24" on each side of the frame assembly, and check for square.

Photo 8 Countersunk pilot holes will allow screws to set flush against the wood.

Clamp the workpiece to a bench, sawhorse or other worksurface so the target hole is clear, and drill a ½" starter hole for the jigsaw blade inside the penciled circle, staying at least ½" from the line (Photo 4). Remember, the top side of the game board is facing down here, so if the drill bit splinters coming out the top side you want that splintering to be well inside the circle's edge.

Use a plywood blade and adjust your jigsaw's orbital action to the lowest setting, then slip the blade into the pilot hole you drilled a moment ago. Cut to the line and around the entire circle to free the center of the hole (Photo 5).

With the center of the target hole removed, thoroughly sand the opening and the edges until smooth (Photo 6). I started with #80-grit sandpaper to quickly remove the worst of the splintering, and then followed

up with #100-grit and then #150-grit. The surface of the game board is now complete, so let's set it aside and move on to the support frame.

Cut the frame workpieces to the lengths given on the Cut List on Page 38. A miter box works best to achieve reliable square ends.

Arrange the frame on a workbench or table with the ends between the two sides, then measure the sides to find the halfway spot at 24". Place the middle frame piece into position and check for square, then mark the location as shown in Photo 7.

Glue and clamp up the frame. These are all plain butt joints and this project will take a lot of rough use outdoors, so we'll need to reinforce them. While everything's still clamped up, drill countersunk pilot holes – two at each of the four corners and two on each

Photo 9 A pair of screws in the center of each side completes the frame.

Photo 10 Never enough clamps! Tape stretched over the edges of the game board will hold everything in place until the glue dries.

Photo 11 Use a compass to draw cut lines for the curved leg ends.

Photo 12 A scroll saw makes quick work in rounding the legs.

side for the middle piece, as in Photo 8. Once drilled, drive 1-½" to 1-¾" screws into each pilot hole (Photo 9). Since the game will be used outdoors and occasionally exposed to dampness, exterior-grade screws are best.

Now, let's put everything together to complete the game board. Spread glue on the top edge of the entire frame including the middle piece, then drop the plywood top into place, being sure that the reinforced side faces downward. With enough clamps you could place one every few inches all around the board, but that'd take a mess of clamps. Instead, clamp up key points around the perimeter – the four corners and the center on each side – then stretch masking tape every few inches to hold everything in place. (Photo 10). It's not possible to clamp or tape the center, so place a few heavy objects in the middle to press the center of the plywood down onto the middle frame piece.

While the main assembly dries, measure and mark the two legs for cutting. Draw a center line on a piece of 1x3 and use a compass set at 1-¼" to draw the rounded end of the leg as in Photo 11. Measure and repeat for the opposite end. The spot where the compass rests is where we'll drill the legs shortly, so pencil in that location as well.

Trim the leg pieces to just a bit past your lines to make the workpieces more manageable, and cut the end curves. You can use a coping saw or jigsaw (or if you have a band saw in your shop you may want to handle this task there), but I've chosen the scroll saw in Photo 12.

The legs will pivot on bolts where they attach at the top of the game board. The easiest way to set these correctly is to place them in their closed position in the upper corner and clamp them in place. Using your marks as a guide, drill a ¼" hole right through both the leg and the game board side at the same time as in Photo 13. Repeat for the opposite side.

Lay the board upside down and thread 2" carriage bolts through the holes from the outside, add a washer and top with a wing nut (Photo 14).

Sand the top and sides, and then apply the coating of your choice. I've chosen a couple coats of clear satin polyurethane varnish, which protects the board and adds a bit of slickness so the cornhole bags slide freely when tossed. You can paint the board any color scheme you like, but gloss or semigloss paint is best.

Speaking of the playing bags, you can readily find these at a large sporting goods store or through online merchants. If you elect to make your own they should be made of duck or light canvas material, and measure 6" x 6" when finished. Fill each bag with a pound of dried corn, beans, or other similar material. Each player uses four bags so make at least two sets of four in different colors.

I designed this game board to keep weight and cost down, but if that's not a consideration you can save a few steps in the building process. Instead of ¼" plywood reinforced around the target hole, you could use ½" plywood. In this case you can skip the reinforcement steps.

For a final bit of customization, you may wish to attach carrying handles to one of the sides. A pair of evenly spaced cabinet door handles screwed directly into the sides will work well.

To learn more about the history of cornhole, regional competitions and rules variations, visit the website of the American Cornhole Organization at www.americancornhole.com, or the American Cornhole Association at www.playcornhole.org.

Photo 13 Drill the pivot holes for the legs with them clamped into place inside the top corners of the game board.

Photo 14 Wing nuts on each side can be tightened to hold the legs securely in either the open or closed position.

Jacob's Ladder

When I was a kid I was fascinated by a toy called Jacob's Ladder, although I didn't know at the time that's what it was called. My name for them was "tumble blocks," and it's easy to see why I thought that. When held by one of the end blocks and dangled, the blocks hang down in a straight line. Tilt that top block forward and over, and each block in turn flips all the way down, clacking delightfully as they go. Tilt that top block back the other way and the blocks flip all the way down again.

The Jacob's Ladder has been a popular toy for a few centuries (*Scientific American* published an article on it back in 1889), but don't ask me to explain how it works; I can't. What I do know is that if you attach the ribbons to six blocks in the right spots the tumbling action works all on its own, which is enough explanation for me.

To make one you'll need a piece of ½" thick by 2-½" wide stock; any standard ½ x 3 material, which is really 2-½" wide, will do. I chose poplar because I like the sharper clacking sound you get from hardwood, but pine clacks fine.

Jacob's Ladder Cut List

Overall dimensions extended: 2-½" wide x ½" thick x 24-¼" long; stacked: 2-½" wide x 4" long x 3-1/8" high

Ref	Qty.	Part	Stock	Thick	Width	Length
A	6	Block	Poplar	½"	2-½"	4"

Additional Materials

#6 x ½" tacks (18 needed)

½" or ⅝" ribbon (3 pieces needed, approximately 30" each)

High-tack craft glue

Photo 1 Sand each block smooth and use the sanding block to lightly round all edges.

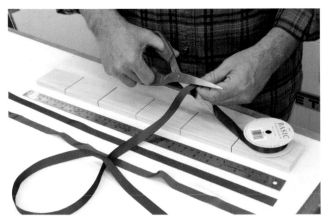

Photo 2 Cut three ribbons, allowing several extra inches for each.

Photo 3 Glue the single center ribbon to the first block.

Photo 4 Tack the center ribbon into place.

Building Jacob's Ladder

Cut six 4" pieces by your preferred method, then give them a good sanding (Photo 1). Start with #100-grit paper, then bump up to #150- or #180-grit to make them nice and smooth. Round over all the sharp edges a bit, particularly on the ends so they'll tumble freely without snagging on one another.

Combining the length of the six 4" blocks and accounting for a slight gap between them, the ladder is slightly over 24" long. Cut three pieces of ½" or ⅝" ribbon to about 30" to give you plenty of working length, as in Photo 2. We'll trim off any extra later. I chose blue for the outer ribbons and red for the center one, but get any color ribbon you like.

To get the hinging action between the blocks correct, attach the ribbons in order beginning with the bottom block. Start by attaching the end of the center ribbon – the red one in these photos – to the center of the bottom block as in Photo 3. Use a high-tack craft glue to position the ribbon. High-tack glue has a very short open time and grabs hold very quickly, which simplifies assembly.

Hold the ribbon firmly in place for about half a minute, then secure it permanently with a #6 x ½" tack (Photo 4). Be careful when working with tacks. They're extremely sharp.

Flip the block over and attach the two outer ribbons (blue here) with glue and tacks in the same manner,

Photo 5 Flip the first block over, then glue and tack the two outer ribbons into place.

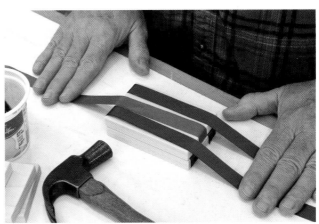

Photo 6 Lay the first block flat, and fold the ribbons over the top.

Photo 7 Lay the second block atop the first, and apply glue on the ends above the ribbons.

Photo 8 Fold the ribbons up and over the second block and press them into the fresh glue.

taking care that the ribbons go the same direction (Photo 5). By the way, in these photos you'll notice that I've got the glue upside down in a small cup. That's because craft glue is very thick, and keeping it upside down in the cup keeps the glue ready to go at the top of the bottle. Much easier than shaking it down every time.

With the ribbons attached, lay the first block on your worksurface and fold the ribbons over the top as in Photo 6. Now, place the second block atop the folded ribbons on the first and apply glue on the ends just above the three ribbons below the new block, as shown in Photo 7. That'll be one dab of glue on the end over

the center ribbon, and two dabs on the end with the two outer ribbons. Fold those ribbons up and press them into the glue, holding them in place for about 30 seconds so the glue can grab (Photo 8). When folding the ribbons up, do so lightly. The blocks need a bit of wiggle room between them to function properly, so you don't want to pull them tight.

Upend the stack and tack the center ribbon into place as in Photo 9, then flip the stack and do the same with the outer ribbons on the other end (Photo 10).

From this point forward it's just a matter of repeating the steps and building the stack. With the ribbons tacked

Photo 9 Once the glue has had a chance to grab, upend the blocks and tack the center ribbon securely.

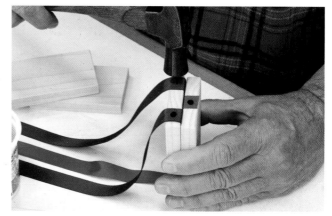

Photo 10 Flip the two blocks over, then glue and tack the outer ribbons into place as before.

on the second block, lay the stack down as before, fold the ribbons over the top, lay the third block into place and dab glue at the ribbon attachment points. If you compare Photo 11 with the similar step shown in Photo 7, you can see that the ribbons are now oriented in the opposite direction – the center ribbon goes to the left here and the outer ones to the right. This should alternate as you work your way up the stack and is a good way to keep track of those ribbons. With the glue applied, fold the ribbons up and press them into the glue, then follow with tacks as before and the third block is complete.

Now, just add the fourth, fifth and sixth blocks, repeating the process of gluing and tacking the ribbons in place each time. When you've reached the top of the stack and have the ribbon secured to the last block, trim the excess ribbon with scissors (Photo 12).

Kids can customize the Jacob's Ladder in a number of ways. Changing the ribbon color is an obvious option, but you can also paint the blocks a variety of colors before assembly begins. Alternating colors on one side to the other completely changes the look of the ladder as the blocks tumble. If your kids are into art – and what kids aren't? – they can draw or paint designs, animals or anything else they like on the faces. I recently saw an interesting Jacob's Ladder where the young builder applied stick-on photos of all the Harry Potter villains on one side, and the Potter good guys on the other. Tumbling the blocks changed the ladder from the Dark Arts to Good Magic with the flip of the wrist.

Photo 11 Fold the ribbons over the top, then lay the third block atop the second and apply glue as before.

Photo 12 Once the stack is complete, trim the ribbons flush with the top block.

Fantasy Sword

Wherever swashbuckling happens – a pirate ship, the fantasy lands of Middle Earth, Sherwood Forest, the deep jungle, or the Roman Coliseum – the swashbuckler's tool of choice is a trusty sword. It's no wonder that kids have enjoyed play sword fights for ages, sometimes using whatever stick they can find. Here's a sword that's impressive to behold, easy to make, and way better than a stick.

One of the most common swords throughout history is based on the Roman gladius – used by gladiators, as the name implies – and variations of the gladius pop up in numerous countries and historical eras. Although different cultures had their own names for it, they all fall under the description of a "shortsword," and were used

by armies worldwide right through the 20th century. The project sword is based on a Model 1832 U.S. Infantry Sword, which you can see in the photo above. It fell out of favor with infantry, but was popular with artillery soldiers on both sides of the Civil War.

To design this sword project I traced a real Model 1832, but made two small alterations. First, I blunted the tip considerably, leaving just the suggestion of a point on it. Second, I shortened the sword slightly so it would fit on a single piece of ¼" x 6" x 24" oak, a common size you can find at most home centers. Hardwood is a must for this project, but poplar or maple would make as great a sword as oak does.

Fantasy Sword

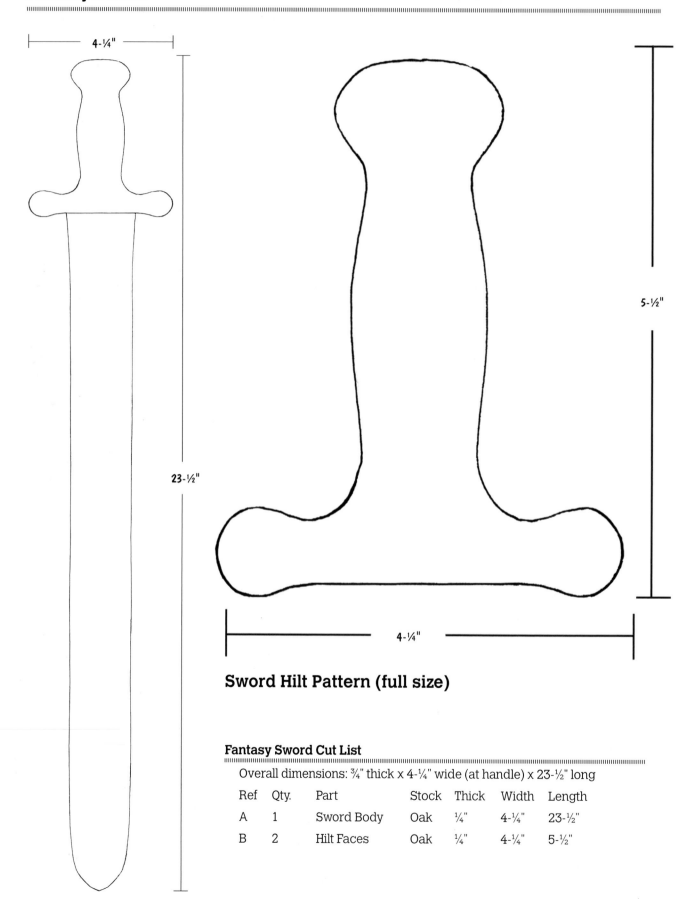

4-¼"

23-½"

5-½"

4-¼"

Sword Hilt Pattern (full size)

Fantasy Sword Cut List

Overall dimensions: ¾" thick x 4-¼" wide (at handle) x 23-½" long

Ref	Qty.	Part	Stock	Thick	Width	Length
A	1	Sword Body	Oak	¼"	4-¼"	23-½"
B	2	Hilt Faces	Oak	¼"	4-¼"	5-½"

Photo 1 Apply spray adhesive to the back of the sword pattern.

Photo 2 Press the pattern onto the workpiece, smoothing it out to remove wrinkles.

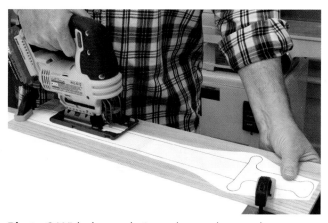

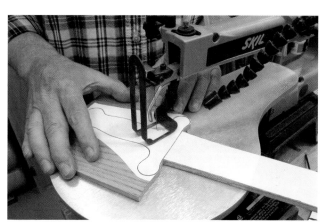

Photo 3 With the workpiece clamped securely, cut out the straightest portions of the pattern with a jigsaw.

Photo 4 For the tightly curved sword hilt, a scroll saw will do a better job than the jigsaw.

Building the Fantasy Sword

Create a Sword Pattern based on the one on Page 48 (also available for download at PopularWoodworking. com/HamlerBook) and apply spray adhesive to the back of it as in Photo 1. Go easy with the spray because you don't need a lot for a secure bond. Apply the pattern directly to the workpiece sticky-side down, and smooth the paper out with your hand so it sticks firmly without wrinkles (Photo 2).

You could cut the entire thing out with a coping saw, but that could be tedious, so we'll combine two tools for this cutting process. Clamp the workpiece lengthwise to a bench or worksurface with one side of the pattern overhanging the bench edge, and cut out the blade portion with a jigsaw (Photo 3). You'll need to unclamp and flip the workpiece around to get the other side.

With the blade cut, move over to the scroll saw for the more intricate hilt, as shown in Photo 4. As you make both of these cuts, work close to the pattern line but not quite all the way up to it. We'll refine all the edges by sanding later (Photo 5).

Peel off the paper pattern. If you were judicious with the spray adhesive it should come right off. If not, dab the paper with a rag dipped in mineral spirits. The solvent will soak right through the paper and loosen the adhesive. With the pattern off, clean up any adhesive residue with the rag and a small amount of mineral spirits. Be careful handling the sword right now, as those two horizontal extensions on the hilt are short grain and easily could break off. That will be corrected shortly.

Copy and print out two copies of the Sword Hilt Pattern from Page 48, and apply spray adhesive to the

Photo 5 Saw just shy of the line; sanding will refine all the curves.

Photo 6 Once the sword main body is ready, cut out two copies of the hilt pattern.

Photo 7 Apply glue to the sword hilt cutouts and clamp up the sword until the glue dries.

back as before. Stick the pattern to your stock, but this time orient the pattern so the grain goes crosswise under it. Cut out the two hilt pieces on the scroll saw as before, or with a coping saw (Photo 6). In the background of this photo you can see how the grain goes side-to-side on the pattern.

Assemble the sword by applying glue to the back of each hilt piece and sandwich it on the hilt portion of the main sword body, then clamp everything up as in Photo 7.

Combining the lengthwise grain on the sword body with cross-grain hilt pieces creates a very strong hilt. This is the same principle behind plywood, where the grain of each layer goes 90° to the adjacent layers.

When the glue has dried, give the sword a good sanding all around. You can do all the sanding by hand, but a rotary tool fitted with a small sanding drum works great for the curved hilt (Photo 8). If you have a spindle sander in your shop, you can take advantage of it for this task. For all the straight portions a sanding block like the one in Photo 9 is the best bet. Be sure to round over all sharp edges of the blade, as well as the sword tip.

You can put the sword to work – or to battle – immediately, but if you wish you can paint it in metallic colors. If you really want to be creative, adorn the hilt with beads or jewels from the craft store. I like the look of the natural grain so I've given my sword three coats of clear satin polyurethane varnish.

As your child plays with the sword, examine it periodically for damage. If edges begin to splinter or get ragged, give the rough spots a good sanding back to smooth, and repaint or varnish as needed.

Photo 8 A rotary tool outfitted with a sanding drum quickly smooths the curved sections of the sword.

Photo 9 Use a sanding block for the faces and straight edges of the sword, rounding over all sharp edges.

Trebuchet

They were called "siege engines," the generic term for any war machine that hurled projectiles before the invention of gunpowder gave way to cannons. There were a few types, and while the catapult is probably more familiar, the trebuchet (treb-yoo-shet) was an improved siege engine that used the power of gravity to do its work. By changing the amount of weight used, along with refining when the sling would release, a trebuchet could be adjusted quickly in the field for both distance and accuracy.

Trebuchets were sometimes unbelievably huge; some weighed tons and stood a few stories tall. They were so big they usually were built on-site during the siege of a

castle or other stronghold. There were smaller ones on wheels, but the big ones were the most effective.

This trebuchet project, like the originals, features a long arm beam and sling. A counterweight pulls the beam down on one end, while the other whips a sling around the other side and up over the top. A loop on the end of the sling releases at maximum arc, sending the projectile sailing toward its target.

At first glance at the Cut List, you might think this is a difficult project. Well, there are a lot of parts and details, but everything is basic so don't be discouraged. It will take a bit more time than some of the other projects, but it's really not difficult to build.

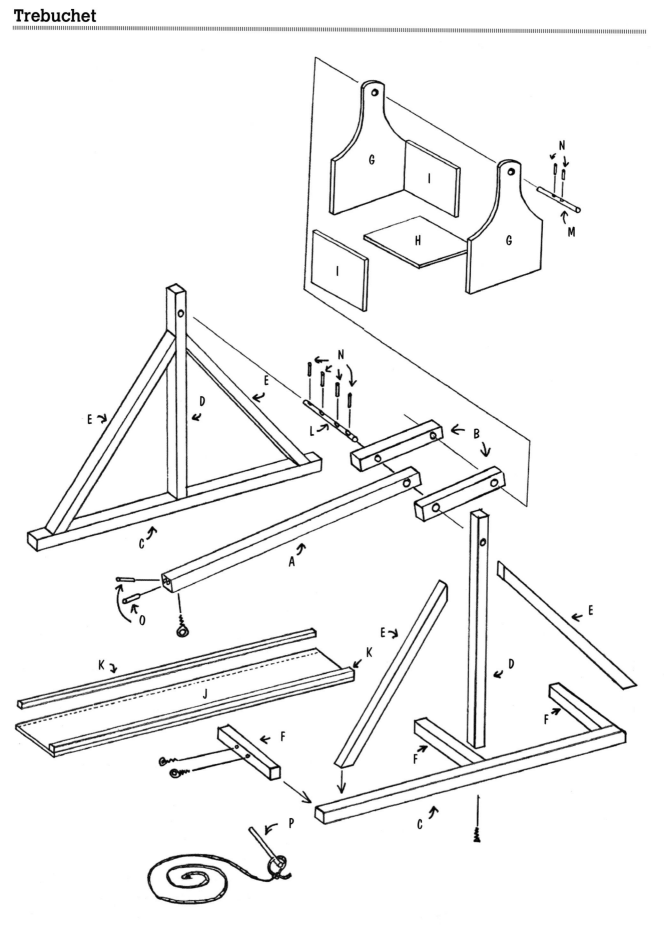

Trebuchet Cut List

Overall dimensions in loaded position: 16" long x 5-¾" wide x 13" tall

Ref	Qty.	Part	Stock	Thick	Width	Length
A	1	Main Beam	Poplar	¾"	¾"	14"
B	2	Side Beams	Poplar	¾"	¾"	5-½"
C	2	Frame Sides	Poplar	¾"	¾"	16"
D	2	Frame Verticals	Poplar	¾"	¾"	10-½"
E	4	Frame Diagonals	Poplar	¾"	¾"	10"
F	4	Frame Crosspieces	Poplar	¾"	¾"	4-¼" (a)
G	2	Counterweight Box Sides	Poplar	¼"	3-½"	5-¼"
H	1	Counterweight Box Bottom	Poplar	¼"	2-½"	3-½"
I	2	Counterweight Box Ends	Poplar	¼"	2-⅛"	3"
J	1	Trough Floor	Poplar	⅛"	2-½"	16"
K	2	Trough Sides	Poplar	⅜"	⅜"	16"
L	1	Beam Axle	Hardwood Dowel	⁵⁄₁₆"	n/a	6-½"
M	1	Counterweight Box Axle	Hardwood Dowel	⁵⁄₁₆"	n/a	3-½"
N	6	Axle Pins	Hardwood Dowel	⅛"	n/a	¾"
O	2	Release Pins	Hardwood Dowel	³⁄₁₆"	n/a	1-¼"
P	1	Trigger Pin	Hardwood Dowel	¼"	n/a	4"

Notes

(a) Only three crosspieces are used in the trebuchet, but a fourth piece acts as a temporary spacer during assembly.

Additional Materials

Heavy string

Thin flexible leather (1 piece, about 3" x 6")

#12 x 1-³⁄₁₆" screw eyes (3 needed)

Photo 1 A miter box and fine-cut saw team up to create perfect 45° angles for the frame members.

Building the Trebuchet

Start by cutting the components to size. As always, I've tried as much as possible to stick with off-the-rack lumber – including standard ¾" x ¾" square dowels for most of it – so you'll mostly just need to cut parts to length. I've used poplar, but any wood species is fine. Your best bet is to use a fine-cut saw and miter box to cut the frame and beam components, all of which have square ends except the frame diagonals. However, a miter box makes cutting these a snap by using the 45° slots as in Photo 1.

Prepare the beam by first marking the main beam at 2-½" from one end. Now, glue the two side beams in place on your marks as shown in Photo 2. This will create a fork shape at one end. Clamp up the assembly and allow the glue to cure.

When dry, mark one of the side beams for drilling per the Beam Detail drawing on Page 54, then secure

Beam Detail (full size)

Axle Detail (full size)

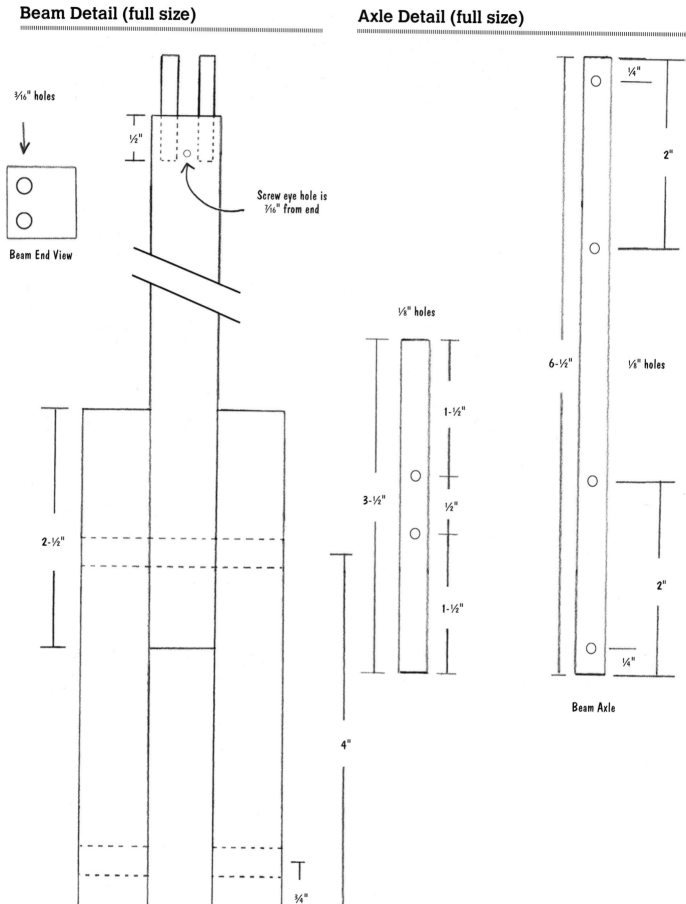

3/16" holes

Beam End View

1/2"

Screw eye hole is
7/16" from end

2-1/2"

2"

3/4"

1/8" holes

3-1/2"

1-1/2"

1/2"

1-1/2"

4"

1/4"

2"

6-1/2"

1/8" holes

2"

1/4"

Beam Axle

Photo 2 Apply glue to the side beams and clamp them to one end of the main beam.

Photo 3 Drill the axle holes in the beam with a 5/16" bit. A piece of scrap between the two sections helps prevent tear-out.

Photo 4 Begin frame assembly by marking the centers of the frame side pieces.

Photo 5 Apply glue to the bottom of the frame vertical, and clamp into place on your center mark.

the forked end of the arm beam in a vise (Photo 3). To prevent the drill bit from causing tear-out, note here that I've slipped a piece of scrap in the gap, and although you can't see it in this photo, I put another piece of scrap right underneath it in the vise. Set the beam aside after drilling.

Measure and mark the exact center of the two frame side pieces, as well as the centers of one end of each frame vertical (Photo 4).

Put a bit of glue onto the bottom of one of the verticals, line up your center marks and clamp it in place perpendicularly to a side piece as in Photo 5. Repeat with the other side. As you make these glue-ups, it's important to check for square and make any necessary adjustments with the clamps.

Photo 6 When the glue has thoroughly dried, countersink a pilot hole beneath the frame side and drive a 1-5/8" screw up into the vertical.

Photo 7 Apply glue to the ends of the frame diagonals, and tape them tightly in place until dry.

Photo 8 Glue and clamp the three crosspieces into place to assemble the frame. Note the fourth crosspiece taped in at the top as a temporary spacer.

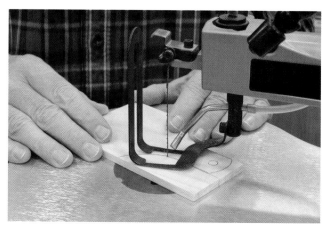

Photo 9 Cut out the counterweight box sides with a coping saw or, as here, a scroll saw.

When dry, secure one upside-down in a vise – or clamp it to the side of your bench or worktable – and countersink pilot holes through the bottom and up into the vertical, which is hidden inside the vise in Photo 6. Drive in a 1-5/8" screw to strengthen the joint, then repeat with the other side.

To finish up each frame side, apply glue to the ends of a pair of diagonals and put them in place to create the triangle shape you can see in Photo 7. You can't clamp these angles effectively, so wrap tape tightly around the joints until the glue dries. You'll find this step much easier if you assemble the sides on a reliably flat surface as I'm doing here.

Assemble the frame by applying glue to the ends of the crosspieces, and clamp them up at the bottom of the frame. While only three crosspieces are part of the frame, the Cut List calls for cutting four of them, and you can see in Photo 8 how I've taped it at the top of the frame – without glue – to act as a spacer and ensure that the clamped glue-up is held square.

While the frame glue-up is drying, move on to the counterweight. Transfer the Counterweight Box Pattern from Page 58 to your workpieces, then cut out the two sides with a coping saw or scroll saw as in Photo 9. Now, clamp each box side to a piece of scrap on your bench and drill the pivot hole with a 5/16" bit (Photo 10).

Photo 10 Drill the axle holes for the counterweight box sides with a 5⁄16" bit.

Photo 11 Glue and clamp the bottom of the counterweight box between the two sides. A piece of scrap acts as a spacer at the top.

Photo 12 When the bottom has dried, glue and clamp the counterweight box ends in place.

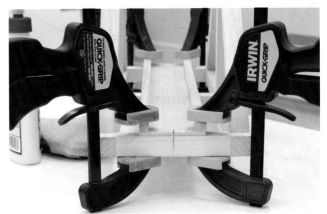

Photo 13 Glue the trough sides into place, then glue and clamp the trough assembly to the bottom of the frame.

Assemble the counterweight box by first gluing the bottom into place between the two sides (Photo 11). To aid assembly, I've used a piece of scrap left over from cutting the box bottom as a spacer at the top of the box. When this has dried, glue and clamp the other two sides in place as shown in Photo 12.

When the trebuchet is loaded, the projectile is placed into a sling, which in turn rests on a long trough or channel on the inner base of the machine that guides the projectile. Create the trough by gluing ⅜" x ⅜" square dowels to each edge of a 2-½"-wide piece of ⅛" stock. I've used poplar as with the rest of the project, but admittedly had a hard time finding poplar in that thickness. If this is the case for you, substitute any ⅛" material for the floor of the trough. Glue the assembled trough to the frame and clamp in place (Photo 13).

Counterweight Box Pattern (full size)

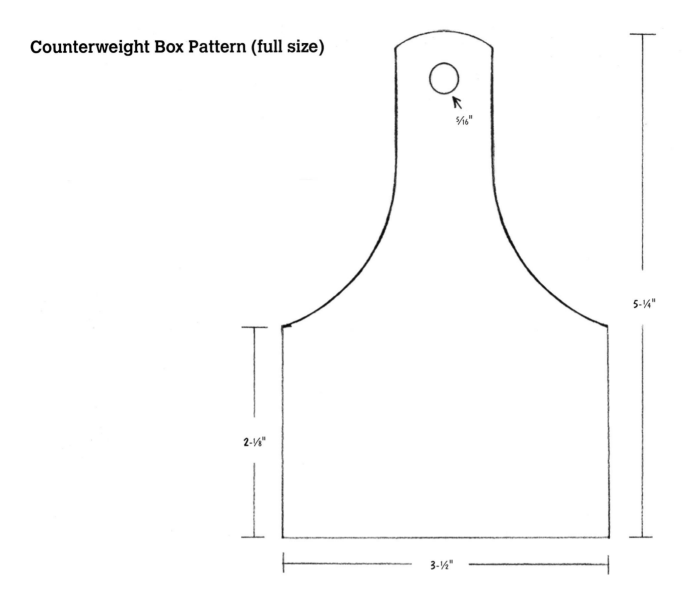

5/16"

5-1/4"

2-1/8"

3-1/2"

Sling Pouch Pattern (full size)

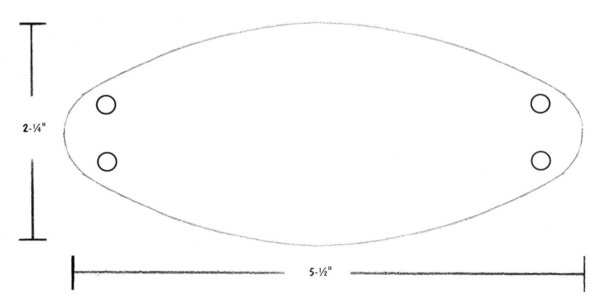

2-1/4"

5-1/2"

Photo 14 Drill ⅛" holes through the beam axle dowel for the axle pins.

Photo 15 With the beam axle in place, secure it with ¾" lengths of ⅛"-diameter dowel pins.

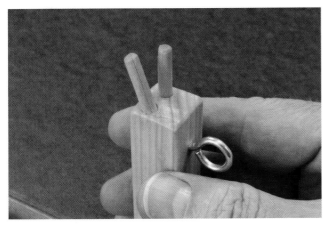

Photo 16 Drill the hole for one release pin straight down into the end of the beam, and the second at a slight angle.

Photo 17 A dowel scrap – or even a pencil – makes a good tool to set screw eyes to the proper depth.

Using the Axle Detail drawing on Page 54 as a guide, measure and mark the beam axle and counterweight box axle dowels. Clamp the dowels securely, and drill ⅛" holes on your marks as in Photo 14. You'll probably have to drill in stages, resetting the clamp to allow access to the whole dowel.

If you haven't already, cut six ¾" long pins from a length of ⅛" dowel. Do a test assembly of the beam by holding it in place and sliding in the axle dowel. If the axle's a bit tight, sand it lightly until it slips in easily. Secure it with the pins as in Photo 15.

Remove the beam and clamp it with the single end upright in a vise or to the side of your bench, and drill a pair of 3/16" holes, each ½" deep, near the top edge. Ideally, the holes should be in the top corners on 3/16" centers from the top and sides as in the Beam Detail drawing. This isn't critical, however, so as long as they're placed near the corners you'll be fine. One of these holes should be drilled vertically straight down into the end of the beam, while the other should be at a 15° to 20° angle. Now, glue a 1-¼"-long, 3/16" dowel into each hole to serve as release pins for launching. You can see what the result should look like in Photo 16.

On the opposite side of the beam, drill a small pilot hole 7/16" down from the top and twist in a #12 x 1-3/16" screw eye (Photo 17). Use a short length of dowel or other thin object to make inserting and adjusting the screw eye easier.

Mark the front crosspiece for the matching screw eyes, vertically centered and 2-⅜" from each side, as in Photo 18. With the beam in place, its screw eye should line up between these two. When the trebuchet is loaded, slipping a short dowel through the three screw eyes secures the beam.

Remount the beam on its axle and check the alignment of the screw eyes. You can tweak this alignment a bit by adjusting the depth of the screw eyes.

Hang the counterweight box by slipping in its axle, then lock it in place with the ⅛" pins (Photo 19).

Use the Sling Pouch Pattern from Page 58 to cut a pouch from a piece of soft, flexible leather. The extended length of the sling is about 10", but cut two strings extra-long to give you some working room. Tie the strings onto the ends of the leather pouch to create the sling. If your leather is very flexible all you'll need to do is pinch the ends of the pouch and tie the string around it. If your leather isn't so flexible, punch a pair of small holes on each side of the pouch as in the pattern, and thread the string through the holes before tying.

Tie one end of the string to the screw eye on the underside of the beam, adjusting the knot so the string is about 9" long, then trim off any excess string on that side. The other string will loop onto one of the release pins at the end of the beam, and you can do that one of two ways. I've chosen to tie the string to a small metal ring, which easily slides onto and off of the release pin. Lacking a ring, you can simply create a small loop on the end of that string. Because this string goes all the way to the end of the beam, it will need to be about an inch longer than the other one to keep the sling pouch even at the other end. You can see a completed sling and pouch in Photo 20. Note that this photo shows the underside of the beam – the sling, pouch and screw eye are all on the bottom of the beam and engage the trebuchet's front screw eyes when the beam is flipped over and down on the opposite end of the machine.

Finally, create a launching lanyard and trigger pin by drilling a small hole in the end of a 4" piece of ¼" dowel. Cut a piece of string a few feet long and tie one end to the dowel.

Photo 18 Twist the screw eyes into the frame so the holes are aligned.

Photo 19 Hold the weight box in place and slide in the axle dowel.

Photo 20 Tie one end of the sling to the screw eye on the beam. A ring or loop hooks onto one of the release pins on the end of the beam.

Congratulations, you've just built your first siege engine! Apply any finish you like – I gave this one several coats of linseed oil, but varnish, shellac or lacquer would all be fine. Of course, you can leave it plain if you prefer.

To load and launch your trebuchet, hold the beam and pouch as in Photo 20. Place the ring, or loop if you've skipped the ring, around one of the release pins. Keep the strings taut and place a projectile in the pouch. I use one of those super-bouncy balls with a diameter of about 1-¼" as my projectile.

Still keeping the sling taut, rotate the beam over the top and down until the screw eyes line up at the front. Place the pouch on the trough at the full extension of the sling. Slide the trigger pin into the aligned screw eyes to lock the machine in the cocked position.

Now add some weight to the counterweight box. Anything at all will do, but if you've got a spare change jar this is a great job for a couple handfuls of coins. I got great results with three or four rolls of pennies. The more weight you put in the box, the farther your projectile will fly.

Ready? Now lean back out of the way – the sling will make a fairly large arc, so you don't want to be leaning over it – and just tug the string to pull the trigger pin. The counterweight pulls the beam down in the back, the front swings up and over, followed by the sling. At the top of the arc the loop string slips off the release pin and the projectile will go sailing its merry way to the enemy fortress.

Which release pin you looped the sling on controls the arc trajectory. On the straight release pin, the sling slips off sooner, sending the projectile on a high arc. In the old days they used this type of trajectory to rain projectiles down inside a castle or fortress. The angled release pin, meanwhile, holds the sling loop a bit longer before it slips off, resulting in a low arc. This was used when a more level shot was desired, for pounding fortress walls.

SAFETY FIRST!

Any toy that fires a projectile should never be pointed at any living thing, only at inanimate targets. This trebuchet can fire a surprisingly long distance, and until you understand its capabilities and firing characteristics it's best to use it outdoors. Always use a soft object as a projectile, such as a rubber ball and not rocks. Using the string to fire the trebuchet keeps you a safe distance from it. Be very aware of the arc the beam travels when slinging a projectile, and don't be in its path.

Rubber Band Racer

There's a Firestone commercial from years ago with a catchy jingle that used the phrase "where the rubber meets the road." They were talking about tires, of course, but there's another place where that phrase is just as true, and that's when you use a stout rubber band to power the drive wheels of this sleek rubber band racer. The size of the rubber band and how taut you make it control how fast, and how far, the car will go.

The body of this racer is cut from a piece of standard 1x3 pine. Photocopy the Racer Pattern from Page 64 (also available for download at PopularWoodworking.com/HamlerBook), then trace the pattern onto the workpiece. You can also attach it directly with spray adhesive, which is what I've chosen to do here.

Building the Rubber Band Racer

You and your kids may find it easier to drill straight holes in wood that's square – I know I do – so drill all the necessary holes before sawing the racer body to shape. The rear 1"-wide opening is curved at the front, so begin by drilling a 1" hole at the front of the opening, which will save time when cutting the pattern later. Now, clamp the workpiece in a vise or to the side of your workbench to drill the axle holes. The rear axle takes a ⅜" hole, while the separate front axles each need ⁷⁄₃₂" holes. Since the spinning rear axle is continuous you'll need a hole all the way through the body. The fixed front axles require only shallow holes into which they're glued, but it's still easier to make this hole continuous as well (Photo 1). This will

Rubber Band Racer

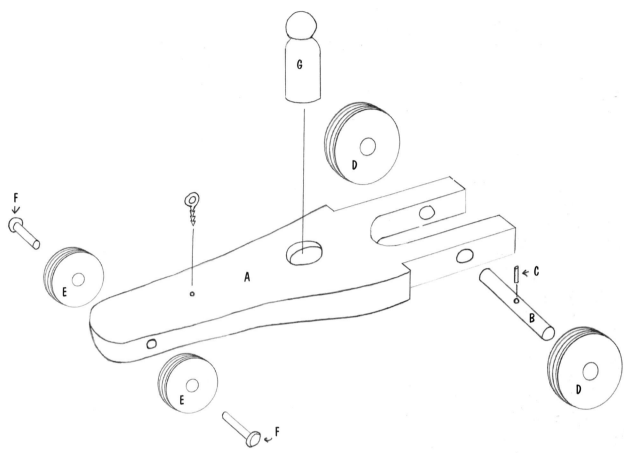

Racer Body Pattern, next page

Rubber Band Racer Cut List

Overall dimensions: 3-¾" wide x 9-¼" long x 2-¾" high (including driver)

Ref	Qty.	Part	Stock	Thick	Width	Length
A	1	Racer Body	Pine	¾"	2-½"	9"
B	1	Rear Axle	Hardwood Dowel	⅜"	n/a	3"
C	1	Axle Peg	Hardwood Dowel	⅛"	n/a	½"
D	2	Rear Wheels	Hardwood Wheels	¾"	2-½"	n/a
E	2	Front Wheels	Hardwood Wheels	½"	1-½"	n/a
F	2	Front Axles	Harwood Axles	⁷⁄₃₂"	n/a	n/a (a)
G	1	Driver	Hardwood Doll	⅝"	n/a	1-⅝" (b)

Notes

Parts D, E, F and G may vary slightly depending on where you get them. Adjust project measurements accordingly.

(a) Usually sold as "Toy Axles" or something similar.

(b) Usually sold as "Wooden Doll" or "Wooden People" or something similar.

Additional Materials

Rubber band (1 needed)

⁵⁄₁₆" screw eye (1 needed)

Racer Body Pattern

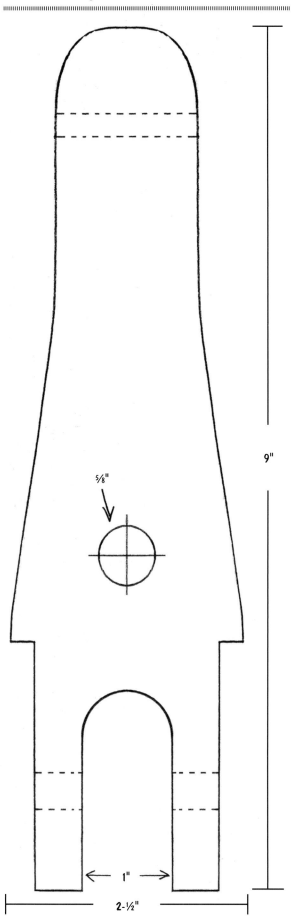

5/8"

9"

1"

2-1/2"

Photo 1 Drill a ⅜" hole for the racer's rear axle, and a ⁷⁄₃₂" hole for the front axle.

Photo 2 A ⅝" Forstner bit or spade bit creates the hole for the driver. Tilting the workpiece makes it easier to drill the angled hole.

also give glue squeeze-out somewhere to go during the gluing step.

The hole for the driver is a little trickier. The large rear wheels make the racer tilt forward, so you'll need an angled hole to keep the driver vertical. The angle of tilt raises the rear of the car about ½", so place a piece of ½" scrap under the rear axle hole and clamp the racer body to your worksurface. With the workpiece now tilted you can hold the drill vertically to bore the hole, and drill straight down without worrying about tricky angles (Photo 2). You don't want to drill all the way through, ⅜" to ½" deep is fine.

You can use a scroll saw to cut out the pattern, but I've selected a coping saw for the task this time. With the workpiece in a bench vise or securely clamped, cut right through the pattern if you've attached it with adhesive, or just follow your traced lines. In Photo 3, I've started with the back of the racer by first cutting the wheel wells on

Photo 3 Cut out the racer body with a coping saw or, if you prefer, a scroll saw.

Photo 4 Sand all the freshly cut edges smooth with a sanding block.

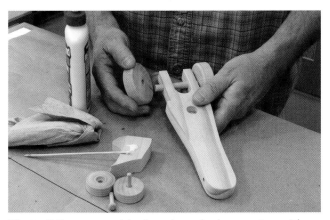

Photo 5 To prevent binding the axle, be sparing with the glue when attaching the rear wheels.

Photo 6 You're sure to get some glue squeeze-out when mounting the rear wheels – wipe it off right away.

each side, followed by the rear opening. Having drilled the rounded front earlier, all you need to do is cut the two straight sides to where they intersect the hole. With this done, reverse the workpiece and saw the curved front of the racer.

With the racer body sawn out, give all the freshly cut edges a good sanding either by hand or with a sanding block as shown in Photo 4. I started with #100-grit sandpaper on my sanding block, then followed up by hand with #150-grit and #180-grit for a smooth edge.

You can find the racer's wheels in just about any craft store, and the good news is that they come in fairly standard sizes. However, as we get ready to mount the rear wheels it's important to note that the wheels you find may vary somewhat from the ones I've used here, so you may need to adjust the length of the rear axle. You want the rear wheels to be about ⅛" away from the racer body on each side when the wheels are glued flush onto the axle, and for my wheels an axle of exactly 3" does

it. Chances are good that the wheels you find will be a match, but just in case, dry-assemble the rear wheels and axle on the racer to determine where to cut the axle and maintain this ⅛" gap on each side.

With the rear axle cut to length, glue it into one of the rear wheels and allow it to dry, then slip it through the rear hole (Photo 5). If the fit is too snug, roll a piece of sandpaper and use it to enlarge the hole just enough so the axle spins freely. Put a bit of glue inside the remaining rear wheel and slip it onto the axle. You'll surely get a bit of glue squeeze-out, so immediately wipe it off while it's still fresh (Photo 6).

To complete the rear wheel assembly, clamp the racer to your worksurface so that the wheels are evenly spaced on each side of the racer body and drill a ⅛" hole ¼" deep dead-center into the axle, as shown in Photo 7. Put a bit of glue into the hole, slip in a ½"-long piece of ⅛" dowel, and allow the glue to dry before continuing.

When the rear axle peg is dry, mount the front wheels. These are a bit different: Where the rear wheels were fixed to a spinning axle, the front wheels spin freely on axles that are fixed to the racer body. For this use ready-made 7/32" toy axles available from any craft store. These are sized to fit standard 1-1/2" wheels (which have 1/4" holes), and you glue them directly into the racer body. Dab a small bit of glue into the front axle hole on one side, then thread a wheel onto an axle and slip it into the hole. Once again you want the wheels to be about 1/8" away from the racer body on both sides. In Photo 8, you can see how I'm maintaining this even spacing by using a wooden coffee stirrer as a spacer. Repeat on the other side.

Finally, glue the wooden driver into the 5/8" hole on the top of the racer.

To prepare the racer's power system, twist a 5/16" screw eye into the center of the racer in front of the driver. The exact spot for locating this screw eye depends on the rubber band you'll be using. To keep the rubber band taut when hooking it to the axle peg, the screw eye should be about 1/2" farther away from the rear axle than the length of your rubber band. My rubber band is 5", so I placed the screw eye 5-1/2" from the rear axle.

Loop the rubber band through the screw eye, stretch it over the driver and hook it to the rear axle peg. Now, put the racer on the floor and roll the racer backward to wrap the rubber band around the axle. When it's taut, just let go to send the racer zooming across the room.

If the rear drive wheels spin in place instead of propelling the car forward, you may need more traction. While the racer should do fine on carpeting, the rear wheels can be expected to slip on smooth floors like tile, hardwood, or laminate. To correct this, stretch a wide rubber band around the center of each of the rear wheels as shown in Photo 9. That'll help the wheels grip on a slick surface.

I like the look of natural wood so I've chosen to give the racer a few coats of boiled linseed oil to let the grain show through. However, this is the perfect project for your kids to exercise their artistic abilities and paint their racer any way they like. For a perfect finishing touch, add some press-apply racing decals and decorations.

One last note – the sizes of toy wheels, axles, and the wooden driver are all pretty standard wherever you get them. However, measure yours carefully and adjust the dimensions of mounting holes or project components to accommodate the parts you find.

Photo 7 Drill a 1/8" hole into the center of the rear axle for the rubber band's axle peg.

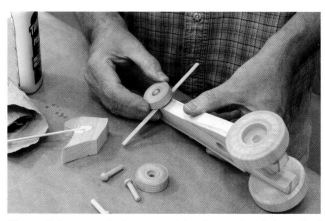

Photo 8 A spacer helps to get the front wheels installed the same distance on both sides of the racer.

Photo 9 A wide rubber band stretched over the rear drive wheels provides traction on smooth floors.

Rubber Band Shooter

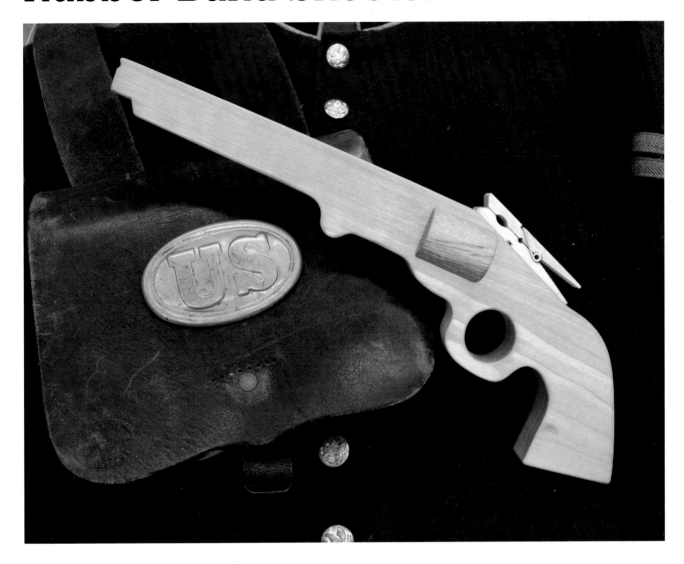

Rubber band shooters like this one have been around about as long as rubber bands. Sure, rubber bands have a hundred practical – and boring – uses, but this project is a really fun way to use them.

And sticking with my not-boring theme, rather than a generic pistol shape for this project I thought it'd be even more fun to base the design on a genuine historical revolver. As with the Fantasy Sword Project, I went back to the mid-19th century for my inspiration and patterned this shooter on the Colt 1851 Navy Revolver. It was a common sidearm during the Civil War for all branches of service, and it was also a favorite of Western legends Wild Bill Hickok and Doc Holliday. That makes it perfect for a backyard Wild West scenario.

Rubber Band Shooter

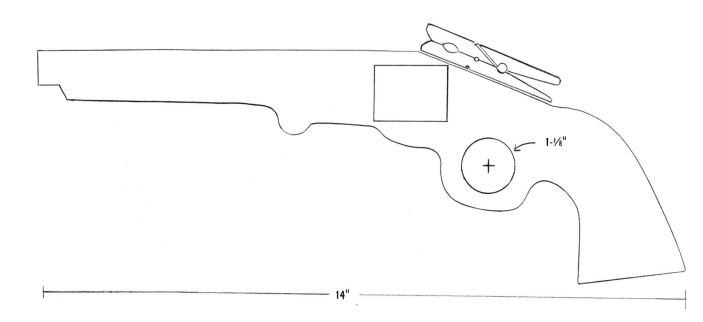

14"

1-⅛"

Rubber Band Shooter Cut List

Overall dimensions: 1-⅞" thick (including cylinder) x 5-¼" wide (including clothes pin) x 14" long

Ref	Qty.	Part	Stock	Thick	Width	Length
A	1	Pistol Body	Poplar	¾"	4-¾"	14"
B	2	Cylinder Halves	Hardwood Dowel	1-⅛"	n/a	1-½"

Additional Materials

Standard wooden spring clothespin (1 needed)

SAFETY FIRST!

Any toy that fires a projectile, especially one as easily aimed as the Rubber Band Shooter, should never be pointed at any living thing. This means no shooting at friends, pets or siblings. (Not even my crazy neighbor.) Use the shooter to fire rubber bands only at inanimate targets.

Photo 1 Transfer the pattern to your workpiece, and mark the center point of the trigger hole with an awl.

Photo 2 Drill a 1-⅛" hole for the trigger hole. The scrap beneath the workpiece prevents splintering on the back of the pattern.

Photo 3 A scroll saw makes fast work of cutting out the shooter, but you could also use a coping saw.

Photo 4 Cut a 1-⅛" dowel right down the middle to create the shooter "cylinder."

Building the Rubber Band Shooter

You can use any type of wood for the shooter. Pine would be a fine choice, but I chose poplar because it is a bit more durable. Begin by transferring the Shooter Pattern from Page 68 to the workpiece (full-sized pattern available for download at PopularWoodworking.com/HamlerBook). In Photo 1, I've just cut out the pattern and traced around it, but you could use a spray adhesive to attach the pattern directly to the wood, the same way as in the Fantasy Sword and Rubber Band Racer projects. With the pattern in place, press an awl into the center of the trigger hole to make a guide for drilling.

With a piece of scrap underneath, clamp the workpiece to your bench and drill the trigger hole with a 1-⅛" Forstner or spade bit, as shown in Photo 2. The scrap underneath the workpiece keeps the wood from splintering or tearing out on the underside, and also protects your worksurface from damage.

Cut out the pattern on the scroll saw as in Photo 3, or with a coping saw. A band saw might be intimidating for children, but if you have one you could handle the cutting chores on it yourself. With the shooter pattern cut out, give the workpiece a good sanding to smooth the freshly cut edge and to round over any sharpness around the edges. A sanding block with #100-grit paper will work well for this.

The shooter already has the exact shape of the historic Colt revolver I used to create the pattern, but you can make it look a bit more authentic by simulating the revolving cylinder on the sides of the shooter body. Do this by securing a 1-⅛" dowel into a vise or clamping it to the edge of a workbench or table, and saw it right down the middle (Photo 4). Make this cut deep enough so you can then place the dowel into a miter box and crosscut a pair of 1-½" half-dowels.

Photo 5 Glue the dowel halves in place on each side of the shooter.

Photo 6 Use a round file to form a small notch for the rubber band to hook into.

Photo 7 Glue and clamp the clothespin into place and allow to dry thoroughly.

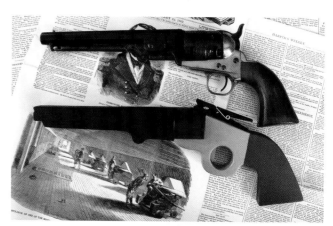

Photo 8 You can leave the shooter plain, or paint it to more closely match a real Colt revolver.

Put a bit of glue onto the back of one dowel half and press it into place as indicated on the Shooter Pattern (Photo 5). Hold the dowel in place for about half a minute to let the glue begin to set, then clamp it to dry. Repeat with the other side of the shooter.

The shooter is loaded by hooking a rubber band on the front of the barrel, so to give it a place to securely seat, make a shallow notch across the front of the shooter with a round file as shown in Photo 6. If you don't have a round file, tightly roll a piece of sandpaper around a thin dowel and use it the same way.

A wooden spring-type clothespin holds the rubber band in place and also acts as the firing lever. Pry a clothespin apart – the metal spring will likely stay on one half or the other – then glue the half with the spring onto the back of the shooter per the pattern and clamp it securely in place (Photo 7). When the glue has dried,

reassemble the clothespin by slipping the free half into the spring and your shooter is ready to go. With the rubber band in place, gently press the end of the clothespin to release it and send it shooting across the room.

In the opening photo you can see that I've left the wood plain. To darken the wood and protect it from repeated handling, I've given it a few coats of boiled linseed oil. However, if you and your young woodworker want to take an extra step you can paint the shooter to approximate the appearance of the original Colt. You can see what this might look like in Photo 8. I've used black paint for all the steel portions of the revolver, gold to simulate the brass middle section, and brown for the wooden handle.

Tabletop Foosball

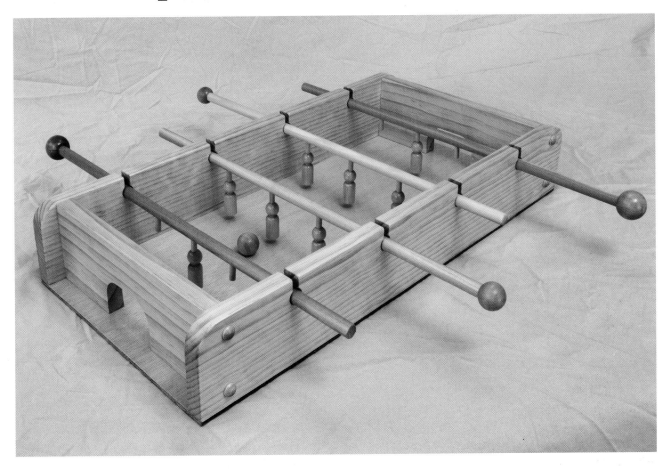

Foosball simulates the field game of soccer, and dedicated foosball tables have been a staple of rec rooms and arcades for decades. Full-size tables vary, but most are around 48" long and feature four control rods and 11 little players per side. However, with a downsized game board and fewer players, foosball is easily adaptable to a tabletop version. For this project we'll cut the game board

to about half size, decrease the number of controls to two per side, and the number of little players to four per team. Your kids will still have plenty of play action, and when they're done the game is easy to store in a closet or under a bed.

Tabletop Foosball

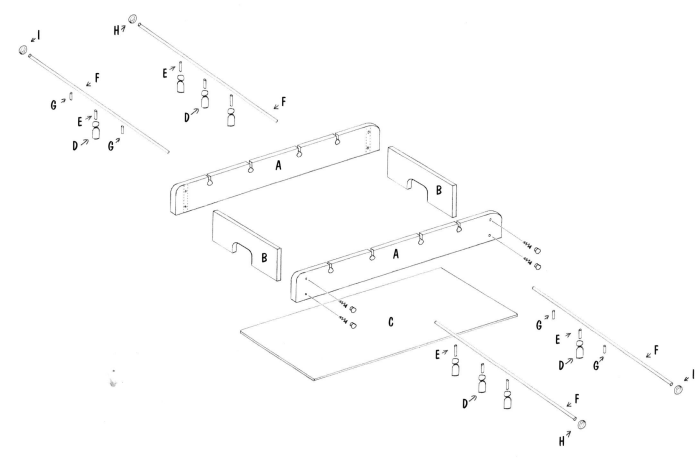

Tabletop Foosball Cut List

Overall dimensions: 11-½" wide x 24" long x 3-¾" high

Ref	Qty.	Part	Stock	Thick	Width	Length
A	2	Long Sides	Pine	¾"	3-½"	24" (a)
B	2	Goal Sides	Pine	¾"	3-½"	10" (a)
C	1	Bottom	Plywood	¼"	11-½"	24"
D	8	Players	Hardwood Doll	⅝"	n/a	1-⅝" (b)
E	8	Player Mounts	Hardwood Dowel	¼"	n/a	1-¼"
F	4	Control Rods	Hardwood Dowel	½"	n/a	20"
G	4	Goalie Rod Stops	Hardwood Dowel	¼"	n/a	1"
H	2	Kicker Rod Knobs	Hardwood Ball	1"	n/a	n/a
I	2	Goalie Rod Knobs	Hardwood Ball	1-¼"	n/a	n/a
J	1	Playing Ball	Hardwood Ball	1"	n/a	n/a

Notes

(a) Parts A and B can be cut from standard 1x4 pine, which actually measures ¾" thick by 3-½" wide.

(b) Usually sold as "Wooden Doll" or "Wooden People" or something similar.

Additional Materials

Hardwood button plugs (8 needed)

Side End Detail (full size)

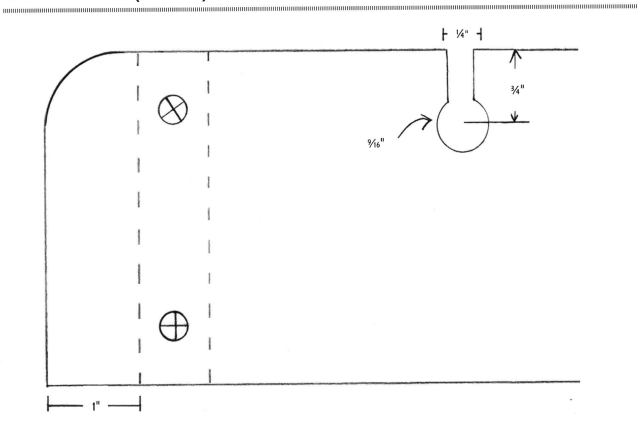

¼"

¾"

⁹⁄₁₆"

1"

Goal Pattern (full size)

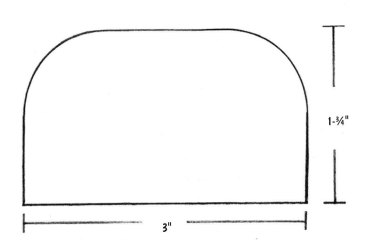

1-¾"

3"

Photo 1 Cut out the goal opening with a coping saw or, as here, a scroll saw.

Photo 2 Measure and mark carefully, then drill the rod holes at the top of the game side pieces.

Photo 3 Create a keyhole by cutting down to the rod hole with a coping saw.

Photo 4 Apply glue to the ends of the goal sides and clamp the assembly until dry.

Building the Tabletop Foosball

The game board is a basic rectangular box with 3-½" high sides, so you can cut all four sides of the game box to length from standard 1x4 pine, which is already 3-½" wide. A miter box is your best bet for cutting these squarely. Transfer the Goal Pattern from Page 73 to the center of the two shorter pieces, and cut the opening with a coping saw, jigsaw or scroll saw (Photo 1).

Prepare the game box long sides by first rounding off the top corners with a jigsaw or coping saw per the Side End Detail drawing on Page 73. Now, lay out the locations of the side holes that will accept the control rods. Measure and mark at 4-½", 9-½", 14-½" and 19-½"; each of these marks should be exactly ¾" from the top edge. With the marks laid out, clamp the sides atop a piece of scrap to your bench or worktable, and drill ⁹⁄₁₆" holes on your marks as shown in Photo 2. Since the control rods are ½", a ⁹⁄₁₆" hole will allow them to move freely without binding.

These side holes are slotted on the top in an inverted keyhole shape to accommodate the mounting dowels of the little players when inserting the rods for play. Mark a ¼" wide slot directly above and centered over each of the holes, then cut the waste free. In Photo 3 I'm using a coping saw, which is really the fastest way to go, but you can also cut these with a jigsaw or scroll saw if you like. Since the player mounting dowels are ¼", cut these slots directly on the line, which will create a slot just a tad wider than ¼". With the ⁹⁄₁₆" hole drilled at ¾" from the top edge, the length of this slot will be a bit shorter than ½". You can see these slotted holes in the Side End Detail drawing.

Fold a piece of #100-grit sandpaper and sand the interior and edges of the slots smooth, rounding edges slightly, then give the entire side a good sanding as well. Repeat with #150-grit paper.

Photo 5 Reinforce the assembly by countersinking pilot holes and driving in 1-⅝" screws.

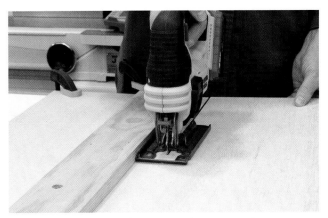

Photo 6 Cut the box bottom with a jigsaw. A clamped-on guide ensures a straight cut.

Photo 7 Apply glue to the bottom edges of the game box, then nail the bottom into place. Be sure to set the nails just below the surface.

Photo 8 Put just a dab of glue around the edges of the countersinks, then tap in wooden button plugs.

Mark perpendicular lines 1" from each end across the inside faces of the long sides. Assemble the game box by applying glue to the ends of the short goal sides and clamping them on your lines between the two long sides, then check the assembly for square as in Photo 4. Insetting the two goal ends gives a playing field measuring 20-½" long.

When dry, unclamp the assembly and countersink pilot holes for two 1-⅝" screws at each corner to reinforce the joints (Photo 5). Drill the countersinks deeply enough so that once the screws are driven in, there's a ³⁄₁₆" to ¼" space above the screw heads. This will give us room to install wooden button plugs to hide the screws.

A jigsaw works best to cut the game box bottom to size. To get a perfectly straight cut, temporarily clamp a strip of wood to the workpiece offset the width of the jigsaw base, as in Photo 6.

Flip the game box upside down and apply glue all around the top edges. Put the bottom into place, aligning the edges all around, and attach the bottom permanently by driving ¾" or 1" brads in through the bottom. Note in Photo 7 that I've penciled a nailing guide showing the center of the box sides all the way around. Be sure to set the nails just below the surface with a nail set so they can't scratch the tabletop while playing. With the bottom attached, give the plywood a light sanding if needed.

Let's go back to those screws in the box assembly and make them disappear. Apply just a dab of glue around the inside of the countersink and tap in wood button plugs, which will cover the screw heads and add a nice detail to the sides of the game box (Photo 8). This is just one way to cover screws with plugs; you'll see another way to do it in the Desktop Bookrack Project on Page 105.

The game box is now complete, so set it aside as we shift attention to the players and control rods. The players are small wooden doll bodies available at any craft store or large fabric store with a craft section, and are the same ones used for the Rubber Band Racer Project on Page 62. These are fairly standard, but for reference the ones I got were ⅝" in diameter by 1-⅝" in length.

The players attach to the control rods by way of short ¼"-diameter dowels, so drill the top of each player using a ¼" drill bit to a depth of ⅜". To make this task easier, create a quick jig to hold the little players for drilling – it'd be nearly impossible to drill them safely otherwise. Drill a few ⅝" holes in a line down the center of a small piece of scrap. Now, use a scroll saw, jigsaw or coping saw to cut the scrap in two right through the holes, creating two halves with partial holes. Place the wooden players in these half-holes, add the other side of the scrap and clamp the two sides together. This forms an assembly that you can now clamp to your workbench for drilling, as shown in Photo 9. I've used masking tape to ensure I don't drill any deeper than ⅜". Depending on how many holes you made in your jig, you'll need to do this a few times to drill all eight of the wooden players.

While you still have the ¼" bit in your drill, move on to the control rods and mark the hole locations. For the center kicker control rods, mark for the three wooden players at 5-½", 8-½" and 11-½". There's only one player on the goalie rods, right in the center. However, these rods need a couple of stops to control how far the rod will move. The kicker rods don't need these because the outer two players act as stops. Mark the goalie rod at 6", 8-½" and 11". Note that the two outermost holes are a bit farther in than on the kicker rod, meaning the goalie has a wider range of movement to protect the goal.

Before drilling the rods, clamp them securely to a bench; if you have a vise, partially open it and set the rods there and clamp from the top. Drill on your marks to ⅜" deep (Photo 10).

Photo 9 Secure the wooden players in the drilling jig, then drill a ¼" hole into the center of the tops.

Photo 10 Clamp the control rod dowels onto a partially opened vise for drilling the player mounting holes.

Cut eight pieces of ¼" dowel to a length of 1-¼" for the player mounts, and four more to 1" for the goalie stops. In Photo 11, you can see how to make this easy. Clamp a small block of scrap to the bed of your miter gauge so it snugly holds a length of dowel in place. Pencil in a mark to indicate the desired length to the side of the cutting slot. Slide the dowel until it touches your mark and cut, then slide and cut again until you have as many as you need.

With ⅜"-deep holes in both the wooden players and the control rods, mounting the players with the 1-¼" dowels will leave ½" of open dowel between them, which will allow the rods to be inserted into the game box's slot holes. Because drilling precise hole depths can be difficult, be sure to dry-fit the players on the rods and check the distance of open dowel – if it's ½" you're golden; if it's not, shorten the mounting dowels or cut longer ones to get the length right.

Dab a very small amount of glue into the top of all eight wooden players and tap the 1-¼" mounting dowels in until they seat firmly as in Photo 12. Now, dab a bit of glue into the player holes in the control rods and tap the players into place. Remember that there are three players on the two center rods, but only one on the goalie rods. With the goalies in place, glue in the 1" dowel stops on either side of the goalie. You can see two completed control rods on the left in Photo 12.

The rods are complete and ready for use, but you can add a nice touch by gluing some knobs on the ends for surer control and an attractive detail. You can find wooden balls already drilled with ½" holes at most craft stores. If they're not drilled, you can drill your own with the same type of jig used earlier to drill the tops of the wooden players. I used 1" knobs for the two center kicker rods. For the goalie rods I wanted a better grip and so glued on slightly larger 1-¼" knobs. You can use either size, or make all the knobs the same if you like.

The last step is to give the entire game a nice finish. Polyurethane varnish is perfect for this, as it not only brings out the grain and deepens the color of the wood, but it also adds a good bit of protection from rough play.

Insert the rods by turning them so the players face upward, and slide them into the slot holes. Once all the way in, swinging the players down into playing position locks the rods in the game box.

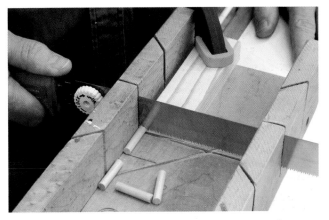

Photo 11 A pencil mark on your miter gauge makes it easy to cut several dowels the same length.

Photo 12 Put a bit of glue into the hole atop the players, and tap the mounting dowels into place.

Outdoor Living

Window Nesting Shelf

I doubt anyone's done a survey on the subject, but I'd bet that if you asked any adult about their first woodworking project, it would be either a birdhouse or bird feeder. And why not? They're easy to make, quick to build, the construction is basic, and they pay dividends for many years. It only seemed natural to introduce both to your kids in this book.

We'll tackle a feeder in the next chapter, but let's begin our back-to-back bird projects by giving them a place to live. This design not only provides birds a home to raise their young, but also gives kids an opportunity to see the process up close. This window-mounted nest shelf attracts three of the most common and people-friendly birds in North America – robins, cardinals and doves. It mounts to a window using a pair of suction-cup hooks found at any home center. With the blinds lowered, as long as you remain quiet and don't make a lot of sudden movements, you can get within inches of a nest full of baby birds.

I've selected Western red cedar for this project for two reasons. First, it's among the most weather-resistant woods around. Instead of rotting, it weathers to a silver-gray patina and seems to last forever. It's also among the lightest softwoods, making it ideal for hanging on a window. There's a third reason which you and your young woodworker will discover as soon as you start working: Cedar smells absolutely wonderful when cut!

Window Nesting Shelf

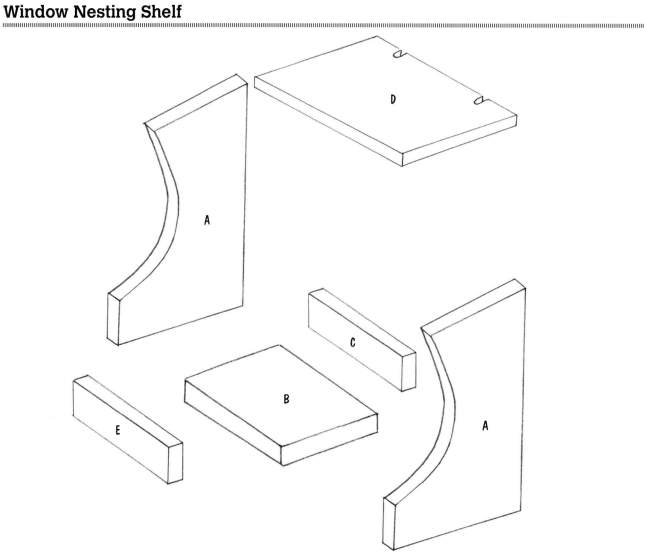

Nesting Shelf Pattern, next page

Window Nesting Shelf Cut List

Overall dimensions (Height/Width/Depth): 9-¾" x 10-½" x 8"

Ref.	Qty.	Part	Material	Thick	Width	Length)
A	2	Sides	Cedar	¾"	7-¼"	9" (a)
B	1	Shelf	Cedar	¾"	6-½"	8"
C	1	Shelf Back	Cedar	¾"	1-½"	8" (b)
D	1	Roof	Cedar	¾"	7-¼"	10-½" (a)
E	1	Shelf Front	Cedar	¾"	1-½"	9-½" (b,c)

Additional Hardware

Suction-cup hooks (2)

Notes

(a) Parts A and D can be cut from standard 1x8 cedar, which actually measures ¾" thick by 7-¼" wide.

(b) Parts C and E are standard 1x2 cedar, which actually measures ¾" thick by 1-½" wide.

(c) Cedar thickness can vary, which may change the needed width for the length of Part E.

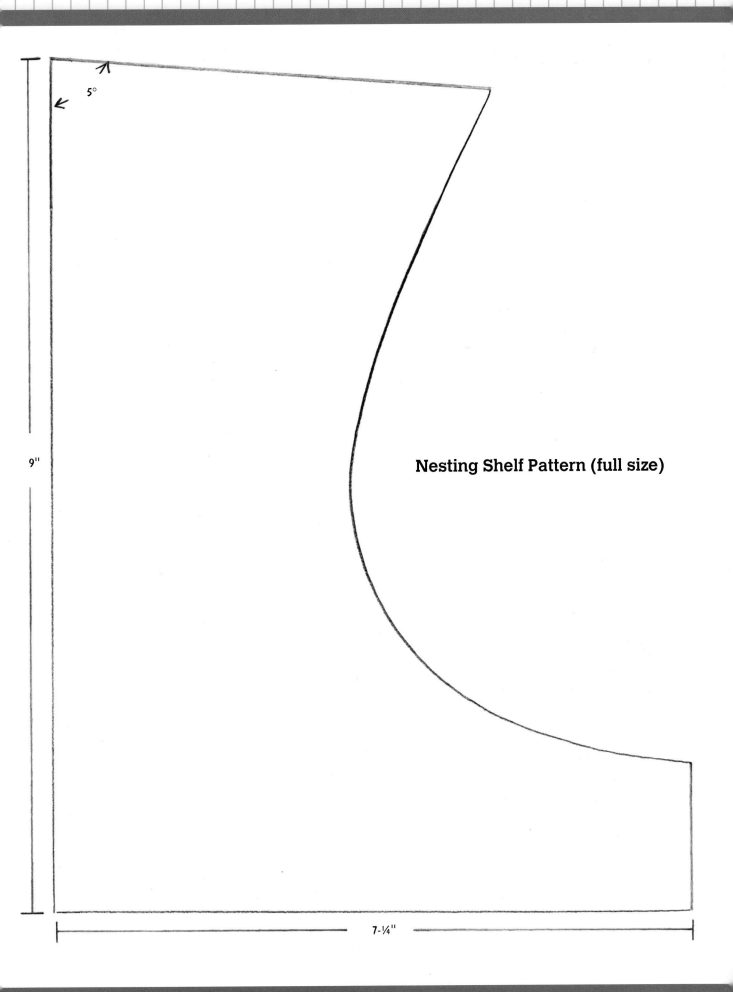

Nesting Shelf Pattern (full size)

5°

9"

7-¼"

Photo 1 Trace the side patterns onto the workpiece, avoiding knots and other flaws in the wood if possible.

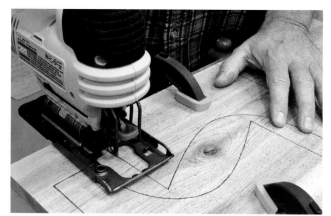

Photo 2 With the workpiece securely clamped, cut out the two sides of the nesting shelf.

Photo 3 Nail on the shelf back. For outdoor structures like this always use water-resistant or waterproof glue and galvanized nails.

Photo 4 Attach the two sides to the completed shelf bottom with glue and nails.

Building the Nesting Shelf

Begin by transferring the Nesting Shelf Pattern from Page 81 (also available for download at PopularWoodworking.com/HamlerBook) to your workpiece to create the two sides, as in Photo 1. Cedar lumber typically has one face smooth and the other rough, and you can orient theses faces however you like. As you lay out the parts for cutting, keep the side orientation in mind for a consistent appearance. I'm using a jigsaw here and for other cutting tasks in this project, but you could use a scroll saw or coping saw for the curved cuts, and a regular handsaw for the straight cuts. By the way, I'm cutting the sides from a piece of 1x10 cedar simply because that's what I had on hand, but I've sized the sides at 7-1/4" so you can cut them from a standard 1x8 board.

Clamp the workpiece to a bench or other stable surface so the portion to be cut overhangs, and cut out the two sides (Photo 2). You may need to rotate the workpiece and reclamp periodically to access all the cut lines.

Prepare the nesting shelf bottom by cutting the shelf and shelf back to size, then attach the shelf back with waterproof glue and 1-1/2" galvanized nails as in Photo 3. Take care that the shelf back is flush on each side with the shelf itself.

Now, attach the two sides with glue and nails, taking care to orient the rough or smooth sides consistently (Photo 4). Set the assembly aside to dry.

Cut the roof to length per the dimensions on the Cut List on Page 80, and secure it in a vise or clamp it to the edge of a workbench. With a coping saw, cut a pair of

Photo 5 A coping saw makes quick work of the two roof notches.

Photo 6 A penciled guideline helps place the nails accurately when attaching the roof.

Photo 7 Use a nail set to drive the heads of the nails just below the surface.

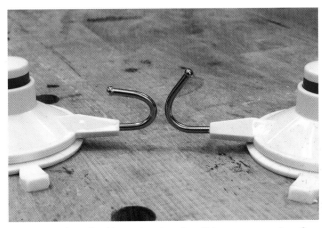

Photo 8 The ideal hanging hook will have an angle of 45°, like the hook on the right.

slots 1-½" to 2" from each end. In Photo 5, you can see how I've started these slots with a drill, which means you only have to make connecting cuts to the holes. These slots should be wide and deep enough to accommodate the body of the hooks you use. In my case, the slots were ⅜" wide and about ⅝" long, but yours will depend on the hooks you get.

Attach the roof with glue and nails, orienting the hook slots to the rear. (Photo 6) Up to now we've used 1-½" nails, but since the roof supports the structure's weight, bump that up this time around to 2" for additional strength. Notice in Photo 6 that I've measured the roof and penciled in lines that correspond with the center of the two sides to accurately locate the nails. I've drawn

these lines really dark for the photos, but make yours as light as possible so they're easy to erase or sand away later.

For a clean look and to minimize exposure to the elements, drive the nails slightly below the wood surface with a nail set, as shown in Photo 7. Do this for other nails in the nesting shelf as well.

Preparing the roof for the hanging hooks is a little tricky, so you may want to handle this task yourself. The hanging hooks work best and the nesting shelf is easiest to mount when the hooks are at a 45° angle. In Photo 8. you can see the hooks I got. The one on the left has a curve that is too sharp; if yours are similar, use a pair of pliers to bend the hook to 45°, like the one on the right.

Robins will gladly nest near windows, like these on my neighbor's window ledge.

Flip the assembly upside down, and from the back drill a 45° hole large enough to accept the hook right in front of the slot you cut earlier (Photo 9). Note here that I've marked the bit with masking tape so I don't drill through the top of the roof. To get the angle correct, you might find it helpful to lay one of the hooks right next to where you're drilling – keep your drill bit the same angle as the hook, and the hole will match the angle of the hook perfectly.

The last step is to attach the shelf front, as before with glue and nails (Photo 10). This front piece is not weight-bearing like the roof, so it's fine to use the 1-½" galvanized nails here.

At this point your nesting shelf is ready to hang; all that's needed is a "For Rent" sign. No finishing treatment is required with cedar. The best place for mounting is a window in a little-used room with not much foot traffic, where you can keep the blinds drawn for the few weeks it'll take the eggs to hatch and the little ones to take wing. For robins, a nest height of 42" to 48" above the ground is as low as you'd want to go; cardinals and doves like it a bit higher.

It should go without saying that once the momma bird builds the nest and lays her eggs, leave the nest alone. Keep all viewing from indoors and create as little disturbance as possible, and you'll be rewarded with the delightful experience of watching the nestlings grow.

Photo 9 To prevent drilling all the way through the roof, mark your drilling depth with masking tape right on the drill bit.

Photo 10 Line up and attach the shelf front with glue and nails, and the nesting shelf is complete.

Bird Feeder

We gave the birds a place to raise a family in the previous project, now let's upgrade the neighborhood by building a local restaurant. Robins won't get much use out of it (they eat mostly insects and worms, not seeds) but any cardinals or doves you attract to the nesting shelf will enjoy a feeder. Same goes for dozens of other birds, especially in the colder months.

As with the Nesting Shelf Project, this outdoor structure is made of Western red cedar that will stand up to the elements. However, the heart of this feeder is a plastic bottle held upside down so gravity lets the seed flow out of the bottle and onto a framed seed shelf. Since the bottle isn't permanently attached it'll slide right out,

so you can take it indoors to refill, something you and your kids will appreciate in cold or rainy weather. Once refilled, just slip the bottle back into the feeder.

You can use just about any kind of bottle, although I recommend plastic instead of glass for safety and because it's lightweight. Any type of bottle is fair game – soda, water, juice – but you'll find that a narrow neck like on a soda bottle works best. You can use any size bottle you wish, but one that holds a quart or liter works nicely. I chose a sparkling water bottle holding just a bit more than a quart. Once you've selected your bottle, be sure to save the cap – it'll come in handy when setting up the feeder.

Bird Feeder

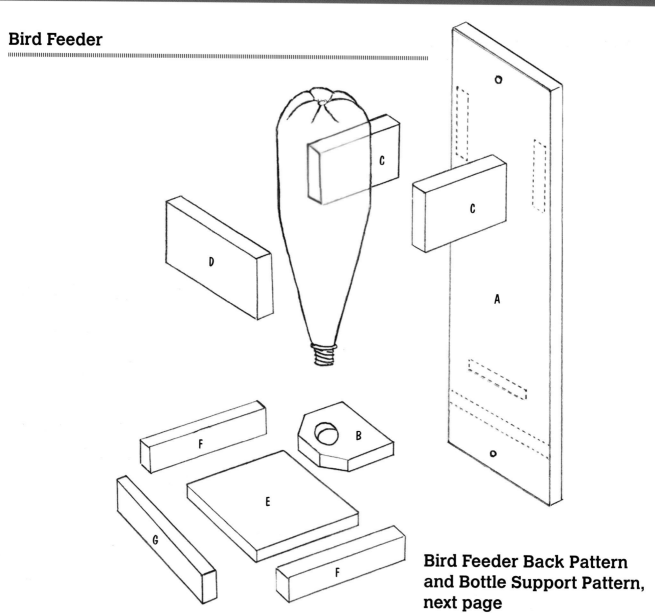

Bird Feeder Back Pattern and Bottle Support Pattern, next page

Bird Feeder Cut List

Overall Dimensions: 7" wide x 5-¾" deep x 14" tall

Ref	Qty.	Part	Stock	Thick	Width	Length
A	1	Back	Cedar	¾"	5-½"	14" (a)
B	1	Bottle Support	Cedar	¾"	2-¾"	3-½"
C	2	Bottle Holder Sides	Cedar	¾"	2-½"	3-½" (b)
D	1	Bottle Holder Front	Cedar	¾"	2-½"	5" (b)
E	1	Seed Shelf	Cedar	¾"	4-½"	5-½"
F	2	Seed Shelf Sides	Cedar	¾"	1-½"	5-¼" (c)
G	1	Seed Shelf Front	Cedar	¾"	1-½"	7" (c)

Notes

All components sized to accommodate a bottle 3-½" in diameter and 10" high.

(a) Part A can be cut from standard 1x6 cedar, which actually measures ¾" thick by 5-½" wide.

(b) Parts C and D can be cut from standard 1x3 cedar, which actually measures ¾" thick by 2-½" wide.

(c) Parts F and G can be cut from standard 1x2 cedar, which actually measures ¾" thick by 1-½" wide.

Bird Feeder Back Pattern

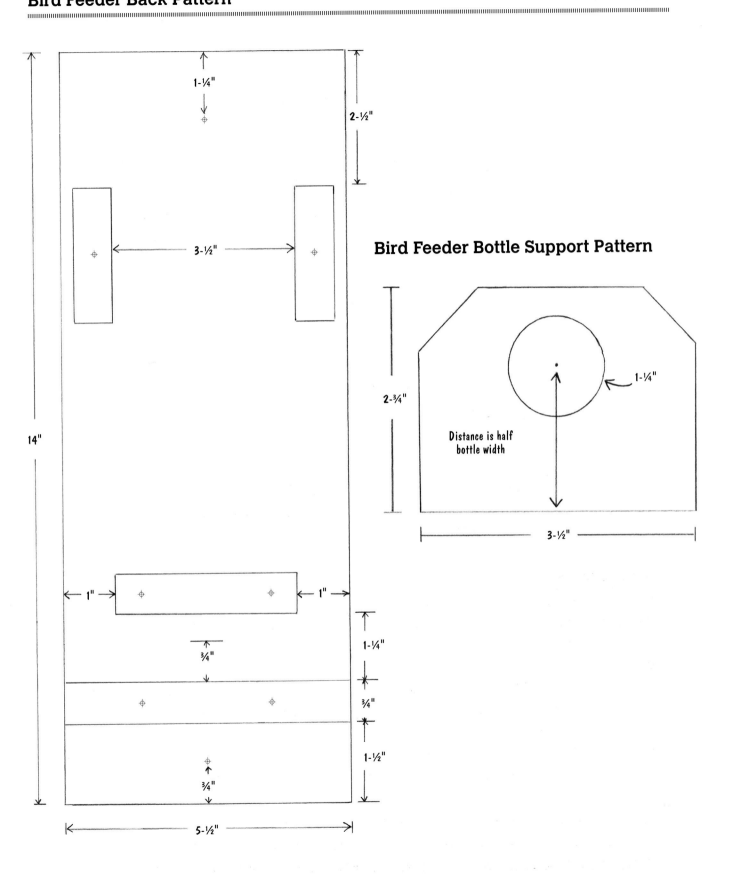

1-¼"

2-½"

3-½"

14"

1"   1"

¾"

1-¼"

¾"

¾"

1-½"

5-½"

Bird Feeder Bottle Support Pattern

2-¾"

1-¼"

Distance is half
bottle width

3-½"

Photo 1 The bottle diameter is the most important dimension when sizing component parts.

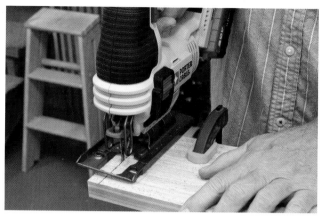

Photo 2 Clamp workpieces securely when cutting to length.

Photo 3 Drill the hole for the bottle support with a spade bit or, as shown here, a Forstner bit.

Photo 4 Clamp the work inside a miter box to trim the corners of the bottle support.

Building the Bird Feeder

Every component in this project is based on the size of the bottle, so begin by carefully measuring yours. In Photo 1, I'm using calipers and ruler to gauge the bottle diameter. The diameter is the key dimension. The top of the feeder is open, so the height of the bottle can vary a good bit without affecting the size of the wooden components. My bottle measured 3-½" in diameter, so the size of all the project components on the Cut List will reflect that. Adjust yours according to your bottle diameter.

Cut the project parts to size per the Cut List on Page 86. With a bottle of this size, the largest workpiece is the feeder back and seed shelf, which you can get from a standard piece of 1x6 cedar (which measures 5-½" wide) simply by sawing it to length (Photo 2).

Prepare the bottle support piece by drilling a hole for the bottle's neck to rest in. Locate the center of the hole exactly half the bottle diameter from the back edge of the support. With a 3-½" bottle, this hole center would be 1-¾" from the back edge. For most bottles of this size a 1-¼" hole is just about right, but adjust yours accordingly. To do the drilling, place the bottle support on a piece of scrap, then clamp both securely to your worksurface. A Forstner bit works best, which you can see in Photo 3, but a spade bit would also work. If you have a drill press, it'll make quick work of the task.

Trim the corners of the bottle support by clamping it into a miter box and, using the Feeder Bottle Support pattern on Page 87 as a guide, saw off the corners as shown in Photo 4. (Bird feeder patterns for this project

Photo 5 The upper bottle holder goes together with waterproof glue and nails.

Photo 6 Do a dry-fit of the components to lay out temporary guidelines for drilling and screwing.

Photo 7 Drill pilot holes in the feeder back piece using your penciled guides on the front side.

Photo 8 Flip the back piece over and countersink the pilot holes from the back.

are available for download at PopularWoodworking.com/HamlerBook). A jigsaw would be a little tough to use for this task because the bottle support isn't large enough to safely rest the saw on, but a scroll saw or coping saw would be fine.

The upper bottle holder is a simple U shape with two sides and a front piece that bridges both. Apply a bit of waterproof glue to the front edges of the side pieces, and then nail the front in place atop them with 1-½" galvanized nails, as shown in Photo 5.

At this point you'll need to do a bit of figuring that will be different with every bottle. Transfer the location for the seed shelf from the Feeder Back Pattern on Page 87 to the back workpiece, along with a small mark to indicate the ¾" distance above where the shelf will be attached

later. Now, dry-assemble the feeder with the neck of the bottle firmly inside the bottle support piece. Locate this assembly so that the bottom edge of the bottle opening aligns with that ¾" mark. When you have everything right, trace around the upper bottle holder and the bottle support piece to mark its location (Photo 6). Once everything is attached and the feeder is vertical, it will support the bottle exactly ¾" above the seed shelf – just right to allow seed to flow out and fill the tray.

Clamp the back piece to a worksurface as in Photo 7, and drill pilot holes for the attachment screws that will be driven through from the back. With the holes drilled, flip the workpiece over and countersink the pilot holes on the back side so the screws will set flush (Photo 8).

Photo 9 Assemble the feeder by driving exterior-grade screws through the back.

Photo 10 Frame the feeder shelf with 1-½" cedar glued and nailed into place.

Start the main assembly by dabbing a bit of glue on the sides of the upper bottle holder and the back edge of the seed shelf, and drive 1-½" to 1-⅝" exterior-grade screws through the back to hold them (Photo 9). Follow this by attaching the bottle support piece in the same manner, taking care it's on the outline you made earlier so the bottle will be held at the proper distance above the shelf.

Frame the seed shelf by first attaching the two side pieces with glue and nails, making sure the pieces sit flush with the front edge of the shelf. Then nail the front into place as shown in Photo 10.

Finally, drill countersunk screw holes for mounting, one at the top and one at the bottom as shown on the Feeder Back Pattern. All that's left now is to locate the feeder anywhere you have hungry birds and fill it with dinner.

The filling process goes more smoothly if you saved the bottle cap. Fill the bottle with seeds, then cap it lightly. No need to twist the cap on tight; it's just going to be there temporarily to keep things from spilling when we upend the bottle into the feeder. With the bottle in position, just reach into the gap between the seed shelf and the bottle and remove the cap, allowing seeds to flow into the shelf.

Now just stash that cap away until the next feeding, and you and the kids are ready to sit back and watch the feeding frenzy begin.

Hiking Staff

This project gives you two great opportunities to spend some quality time with your kids. You'll build the project together, of course, but an enjoyable hike in the woods to gather materials is also part of the package.

Twisty hiking staffs are an old tradition, and it's not difficult to find the perfect stick to work with. To prepare for this project I took a hike on one of my local trails and found two good candidates within 15 minutes. One had a uniform spiral pattern in the stick, while the other was severely twisted for about a foot and a half at the top.

Making the Hiking Staff

These sticks are twisted by vines, with the most common being wisteria, grape and honeysuckle (Photo 1). Fortunately, poison ivy prefers a wider surface to climb – like the trunk of a fully grown tree – and rarely encircles saplings. Still, be on the lookout for those telltale three leaves and if in doubt, move on to a different sapling.

As vines spiral up a sapling they restrain the tree's natural growth. In some cases the sapling remains straight, but as it grows in circumference the strong vine presses deeply into the sapling to create an embossed spiral pattern. In other cases, the vine proves stronger than the sapling, which then grows in a stunted and, sometimes, corkscrew fashion. You can see examples of both types in Photo 2.

Before getting started you may want to put on a pair of light gloves. Working with green saplings, especially when removing the bark, can be a bit goopy due to the sap. Saplings can also leave stain on your fingers, but at the very least you'll find it sticky work.

Photo 2 A quick hike on a local trail turned up two great candidates for hiking staffs.

Photo 3 Remove the bark with a scraper or, as here, a putty knife.

The first thing to do is break off any small branches or twigs, and remove the vine. If the vine is still green this will be easy; it'll probably just unwind like a coiled rope. Dry vines may come off in pieces.

Clamp the stick to a bench or other worksurface, then use a knife or scraper to remove as much bark as you can. This will involve a combination of scraping, pulling and peeling. The removal process varies depending on the sapling – some species peel easily in long unbroken strips like the one in Photo 3, while others have thin bark that you can scrape off.

The sapwood right under the bark is pretty soft, so take care not to dig too far into it. The idea is to just remove the bark to expose the bare wood. As you work you'll notice that the wood is light-colored, but it quickly darkens as the sapwood dries from exposure to the air.

If you're lucky enough to have found a stick where the vine has created deep fissures and caused the stick itself to spiral, you're going to end up with an exotic looking

Photo 1 Vines have just begun encircling this thin sapling. In another year or two it'll be nicely twisted.

hiking staff. However, the deeper the fissures the more difficult they'll be to clean out. Pieces of vine, rotted bark, bits of leaves and dirt can all remain wedged in there so clean out as much as you can. A narrow screwdriver or similar implement works well for this task (Photo 4).

This project comes with an intermission. To sand the wood smooth (and to stain and finish, if desired), the stick should be nice and dry, so once you have the stick stripped and cleaned, store it in a well-ventilated spot. It's not at all necessary, but if your stick is bent you can straighten it a bit during the drying. You can do this by securing it to a length of pipe or just about anything else that is strong and straight. In Photo 5, I've clamped my stick onto the edge of a 2x6, pulling the curves as straight as possible.

There's no real way to predict how long drying will take, as that depends on wood species and thickness of the stick, but let it dry for at least a month. The longer, the better. With my stick clamped into my straightening jig I'll stash it into a corner of the shop and move on to some other projects as it dries.

OK, I'm back. It's been several weeks and with the stick nicely dried I've unclamped it and will cut it to length. Hiking staffs are personal things. Some hikers like them not much longer than a cane or walking stick, while others enjoy a staff that's considerably longer. When sizing the stick, give some thought to where you'll likely grip it. If the stick has a natural twist or bend that would make a good hand-hold, trim the stick so this spot will be at a natural and comfortable height (Photo 6).

My stick has a perfect bend pretty similar to the top of one of my cross-country ski poles, so that's where I'll make the hand-hold and trim it to length accordingly.

Photo 4 A narrow tool, like this small screwdriver, digs debris out of the fissures caused by the vine.

Photo 5 Clamped firmly to this length of 2x6, the sapling will straighten as it dries.

Photo 6 Cut the stick to the length you want.

Photo 7 Use any combination of file, rasp or sanding block to round over the cut ends.

Photo 8 Go over the stick and remove any rough spots or sharp nubs from twigs and small branches.

Photo 9 Sanding smooths the dried wood, and removes any remaining bits of bark.

Photo 10 To create the wrist strap, pass the cord through the drilled hole, then knot it securely.

Once trimmed, round over the ends with a file or rasp, or a sanding block with coarse sandpaper (Photo 7).

Your stick likely has some hard, and possibly sharp, nubs left by small twigs or branches. Get rid of these with a sanding block or rasp, and cut off larger ones with a saw (Photo 8).

Now, give the entire staff a good sanding. Start with coarse paper like #80-grit, then bump up to #100-grit. If you'd like it even smoother, finish with #120- or #150-grit (Photo 9). Pay particular attention to any area that you or your child will regularly handle while hiking, and be sure those spots are very smooth.

Once sanded you can stain the stick with any wood stain if you'd like a darker appearance. You can also apply a clear finish if you'd like. I've not stained the project staff, but I have given it a few coats of Danish oil – an oil/varnish blend – for a bit of protection from the elements. If you'd like more of a shine and even more protection, consider a coat or two of polyurethane.

At this point your hiking staff is ready to hit the trail, but consider one more optional step. You may find a wrist strap useful in helping hold onto the staff while hiking, plus a strap allows you to hang the staff for storage. You can make the strap out of any rope or cord; I've chosen leather.

Drill a hole either just above or just below where you typically hold the staff while hiking, orienting the hole from side-to-side. Now, just slip your strap material through the hole, trim it to the length you want, and knot it at the end (Photo 10). Allow a bit of room here. You don't want this strap tight or confining, you just want it to loosely encircle your wrist so you can keep hold of the stick while hiking.

Kite Winder

When it comes to toys that are absolutely ageless, kites have to be somewhere near the top of the list. On a recent summer trip to Kitty Hawk, N.C., I think I saw just as many adults flying kites on the beach as kids – maybe more. Some of these kites were huge, and the folks flying them sometimes had expensive string winders that looked more like deep-sea fishing reels. But for normal-sized kites, a simple string winder like the one in this project is easy to make and costs almost nothing. It will work just as well for reeling in even the wildest kite.

Kite Winder

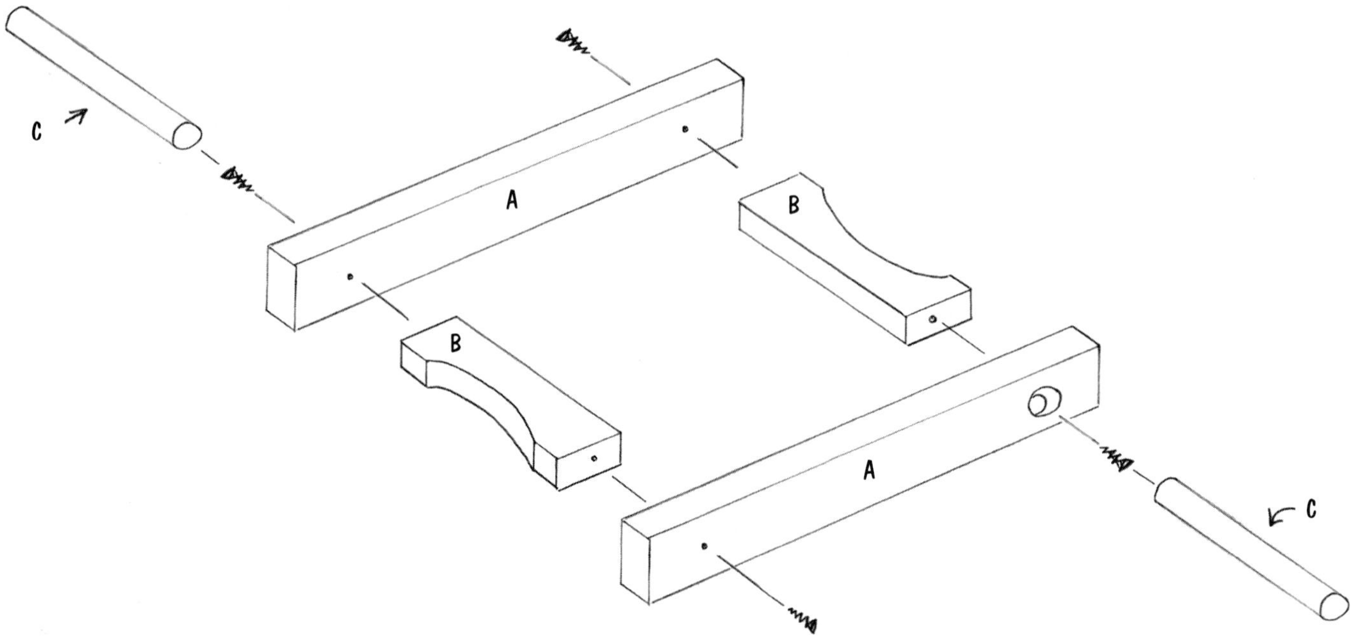

Spindle Pattern (full size)

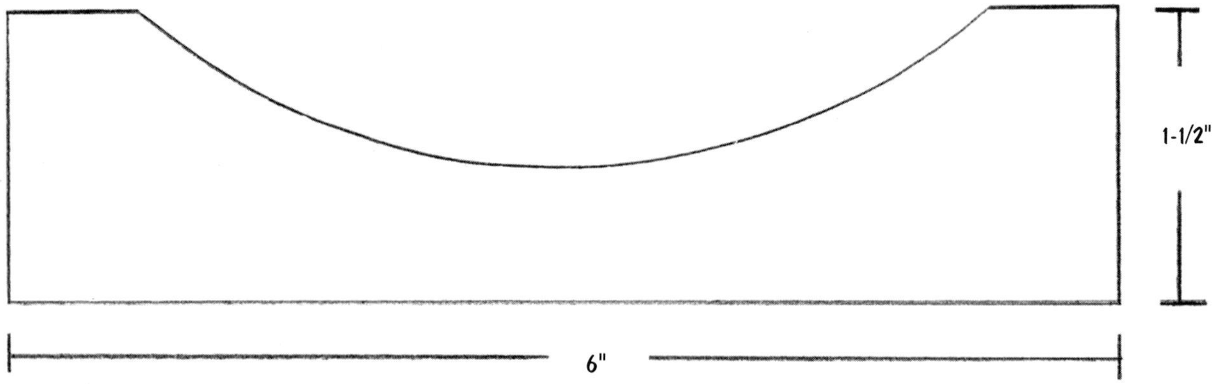

Kite Winder Cut List

Overall dimensions (including handles): 15-½" wide x 10" long x 1-½" thick

Ref	Qty.	Part	Stock	Thick	Width	Length
A	2	Sides	Pine	¾"	1-½"	10" (a)
B	2	Spindles	Pine	¾"	1-½"	6" (a)
C	2	Handles	Hardwood Dowel	¾"	n/a	4-½"

Notes

Parts A and B can be cut from standard 1x2 pine, which actually measures ¾" thick by 1-½" wide.

Photo 1 Cut all the parts except the handles from standard 1x2 pine.

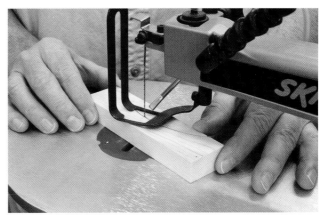

Photo 2 A scroll saw easily cuts the curve in the spindles, but you can also use a coping saw.

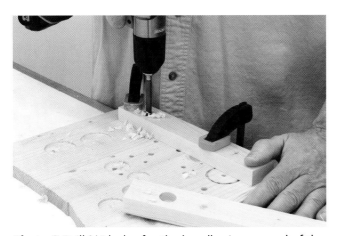

Photo 3 Drill ¾" holes for the handles in one end of the side pieces only.

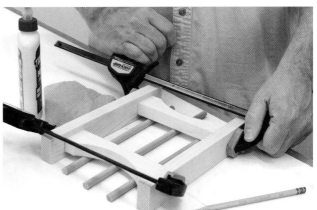

Photo 4 Some ⅜" dowels help to center the spindles during assembly.

Building the Kite Winder

The components for the kite winder are quite basic: just a few lengths of 1-½" pine (cut from standard 1x2), and a couple short ¾" dowels. To ensure square ends, cut the two sides and the two center spindles to length in a miter box (Photo 1).

Transfer the curve from the Spindle Pattern on Page 96 (also available for download at PopularWoodworking.com/HamlerBook) to the two shorter pieces, centering the curve on the edge of each. Use a coping saw or scroll saw to cut the waste away from the curve (Photo 2). Since these pieces are so short they'd be difficult to clamp up and cut safely with a jigsaw, but if you have a band saw in your shop and wanted to handle this task yourself, that tool would turn these out quickly.

Mark each of the two sides 1-¾" down from the ends for the locations of the reinforcing screws we'll add a bit later. Clamp the side pieces atop a piece of scrap on your bench or worktable, and drill a ¾" hole ½" deep on one of the marks on each piece as in Photo 3. There's only one handle on each side, so be sure to drill for only one.

Apply glue to the ends of the spindles and assemble the winder, locating the spindles 1" from the ends of the side pieces. Be sure to orient the sides correctly so that the handle holes are located on opposite ends of the winder. The spindles should be centered lengthwise, which would mean a gap on each side of ⅜", but rather than do a lot of measuring I've simply supported them with a few ⅜" dowels while clamping up the assembly (Photo 4).

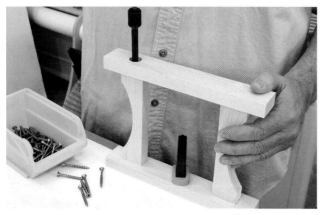

Photo 5 Countersink pilot holes for the screws. One of these will go right in the handle hole on each side.

Photo 6 Drive screws in place to reinforce the assembly.

Photo 7 Give the winder a good sanding all around, making sure to round over the front edges of the string spindle.

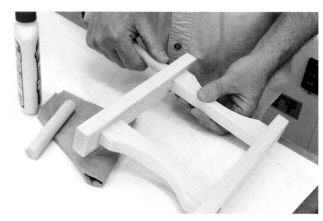

Photo 8 Glue the handles into place on each side of the winder.

When the assembly has dried, remove the clamps and drill countersunk pilot holes for the reinforcing screws. On each of the side pieces, one pilot hole will go right in the center of the hole you drilled for the dowel handles, as in Photo 5.

With the pilot holes drilled, drive in screws to hold everything together securely (Photo 6). Use 1-⅝" or 1-¾" screws for the side without the handle. Since the handle holes are already ½" deep, use 1-¼"screws for those two spots.

Before installing the handles, give the completed assembly a good sanding all around, starting with #150-grit paper (Photo 7). You'll want to round over all sharp edges, especially on the curved portions of the spindles where the string will contact the winder.

Dab a bit of glue around the inside of both handle holes – not too much, or you'll have a lot of squeeze-out –

then set the handles into place with a twisting motion to seat them firmly, as in Photo 8.

The winder can be left plain, but it'll receive a lot of handling so consider applying a few coats of shellac or polyurethane. When the finish has thoroughly dried, tie your kite string around the center of one of the spindles, and then start the wrapping around the curved parts of the two spindles. Once the string is established, just crank the winder until you have as much string as you like and that's it.

Now, go fly a kite.

Noisemaker

It hardly seems that kids need anything else to make more noise, but here's a great easy project to do exactly that. There are occasions – New Year's, school football or basketball games, birthday parties, general backyard mayhem – where making a lot of loud noise is, after all, the whole point.

Because this project is so easy, I thought I might do something a little different this time with a great technique to show your kids, and that's building two projects at the same time. This is a perfect project to share with a friend, and your young woodworker can do exactly that by doubling up identical workpieces to save time and add efficiency. Of course, it's perfectly fine to make just one, but I think once you suggest making one for themselves and a friend, your kids will jump at the chance.

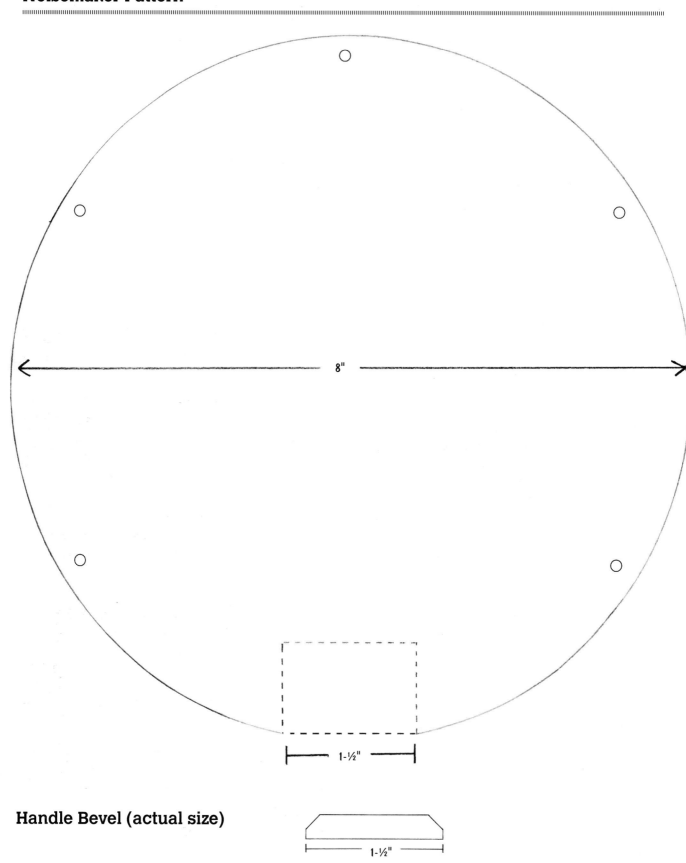

8"

1-½"

Handle Bevel (actual size)

1-½"

Noisemaker Cut List

Overall dimensions (Including Handle): 8" wide x 12" long x ¾" thick

Ref	Qty.	Part	Stock	Thick	Width	Length
A	2	Paddle	Birch Ply	¼"	8"	n/a
B	4	Handle Sides	Pine	¼"	1-½"	5" (a)
C	2	Handle Center	Pine	¼"	1-½"	4" (a)
D	10	Balls	Hardwood	1"	n/a	n/a

Notes

The list above is for two noisemakers; halve the quantities for a single project.

Parts B and C can be cut from standard ¼" x 2" pine, which actually measures 1-½" wide.

Additional Materials

Heavy string or cord

Building the Noisemaker

Start by taping two pieces of ¼" plywood together to create the circular paddle shapes. I recommend good 5-ply birch plywood for this, which you can find at a craft or woodworking supply store; stay away from construction-grade ply this time around. With the pieces taped, draw an 8" circle with a compass. Using the Noisemaker Pattern on Page 100 as a guide, pencil in the locations for the five string holes ¼" from the edge.

Put the stacked workpieces on a piece of scrap and clamp it to your bench or table, then drill the string holes as in Photo 1. If a hole falls right where you've taped, that's not a problem; just drill right through the tape. The size of these holes isn't critical, but a hole of ⁵⁄₃₂" to ³⁄₁₆" should accept most string.

With the workpieces still joined, cut out the circle with a coping saw, jigsaw or scroll saw as in Photo 2. As before, just ignore the tape, it won't affect cutting at all. Note on the Noisemaker Pattern that there's a 1-½" flat spot on the bottom of the circle where the handle goes. You can create this flat spot when cutting, or do it by sanding in the next step. Either way, keep this flat spot exactly opposite the middle string hole on the other side of the circle.

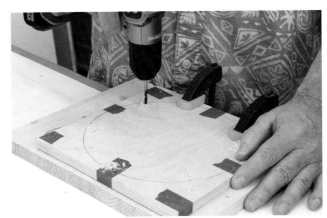

Photo 1 Clamp the paddle workpieces to a piece of scrap atop your worksurface and drill the string holes.

Photo 2 Cut out the stacked paddle shapes on the scroll saw, or with a coping saw.

Photo 3 With the circles cut out, give the edges a good sanding, then untape and sand the faces.

Photo 4 Use a small block plane to shave a bevel on the handle workpiece before cutting it to length.

Photo 5 Cut the handle pieces squarely to length in a miter box. A fine-cut saw like this will ensure smooth, clean edges.

Photo 6 Glue one handle side to the handle center piece with one end flush, then clamp until dry.

You obviously cut through the tape in the previous step, so line up the holes and retape the circles, then give the edges a good sanding to remove cut marks and generally smooth the outside edges (Photo 3). If you didn't create the flat spot in the previous step, hold the stacked circles overhanging your bench or worktable and use a sanding block vertically to make it. You're not removing a lot of material so it will go quickly. Remove the tape to smooth those last few spots, and you now have two identical noisemaker paddles.

We'll make the handles with a beveled edge on the side pieces, but sticking with our theme of making multiples with a single action it's easier to create the bevel before cutting the workpieces to length. Select a piece of ¼" x 1-½" pine that's long enough for four side pieces and secure in a vise or clamp it to the edge of a bench or worktable. Now, run a small block plane at about 45° along one edge, as shown in Photo 4. This angle is just

to ease the edge of the handle and make it easier to hold, so the exact angle isn't critical at all. After the first edge, flip the workpiece over and do the edge on the opposite side. You can get an idea what the result will look like in profile in the Handle Bevel drawing on Page 100.

Beveling this edge is optional. If you prefer you can leave the edge square and give it a bit of rounding over with a sanding block later, or with a small sanding drum on a rotary tool as shown in the Fantasy Sword project on Page 47.

Cut the handle pieces to length – the four beveled handle sides are 5" long, while the two unbeveled center pieces are 4". A fine-cut saw and miter box give the best cuts (Photo 5).

Apply glue to the face of a short center piece and clamp it to the longer side piece as in Photo 6. One end of this assembly should be flush, while the other end overhangs the shorter center piece by 1".

When these have dried, unclamp and apply glue to that overhanging portion and affix it to the bottom of one of the paddles right at the flat spot. Now, apply glue to the inner face of the remaining handle side to create a sort of sandwich with the handle components (Photo 7). Clamp up until dry and the result will look like an oversized ping-pong paddle.

You may be able to find drilled wooden balls at your local craft store, but if not you'll need to prepare your own while the paddles dry. Drilling holes in spheres is tricky, but an easy jig similar to the one used for the Tabletop Foosball Project simplifies the task. To create the jig, drill three or four 1" holes through a piece of ¾" scrap. Now, use a jigsaw or handsaw to cut that piece of scrap right down the middle through the center of those holes.

Place the two pieces on some scrap for drilling, put wooden balls into those holes, and use small clamps to squeeze the two halves together. Bingo, those wooden balls are held fast. Now, just clamp the jig onto a piece of scrap on your worksurface, and drill holes through the balls of the same size you used to drill the paddles (Photo 8). Depending on how many 1" holes you made in your jig, you'll need to do this a few times to drill all 10 balls for the two noisemakers.

To complete the noisemakers cut lengths of string or cord and thread them through the balls and secure the ends with a double knot (Photo 9). Slip the other end of the string into the holes in the paddle and knot it, then trim off the extra string. You'll want the string length after tying to be no longer than 3" to keep the balls from tangling, and to keep the lower two balls from striking your hand when holding the noisemaker.

You can leave the noisemakers plain, give them a clear finish like varnish or shellac, or paint them up in bright colors – the louder the color the better, of course. If you do apply a finish, do it before tying the balls with the string. To paint or varnish the balls, slip them onto a thin dowel or length of cut coat hanger.

At this point your young woodworkers will be eager to share their new noisemakers with a friend – the whole point of making two of them – so your task now is to send them on their merry noisy way over to their friend's house to play with their new toys. You, meanwhile, can enjoy the peace and quiet.

Until they get home.

Photo 7 Glue the first half of the handle assembly to the paddle, then add the other handle side.

Photo 8 Secure the wooden balls in the drilling jig clamped to your worksurface, and drill holes all the way through.

Photo 9 Thread strong cord or string through the drilled balls and tie securely.

Indoor Living

Desktop Bookrack

Infants and toddlers love being read to. When they get a bit older they thrill at being able to look into a book you used to read to them – one that appeared to be nice pictures and a lot of gibberish when they were smaller – and be able to read it back to you … even if they don't get all the words right. But then somewhere down the road they tend to drift away from books as they get older, and that's tragic.

What if, though, somewhere between those two age ranges you could work with them on a project that encouraged them to care for books and keep them close

at hand? And it doesn't matter what kinds of books either – classics, sci-fi, young-adult, Harry Potter or even comic books, anything they like to keep the spark alive is a good thing. That's where this project comes in.

This basic gravity-style bookrack is easy to build and easy for kids to customize: Just change the dimensions to accommodate almost any size or amount of books. For paperbacks you can make it long and narrow, or for an encyclopedia use workpieces that are wide and strong; it's really up to them. And if they can't decide, help them build more than one.

Desktop Bookrack

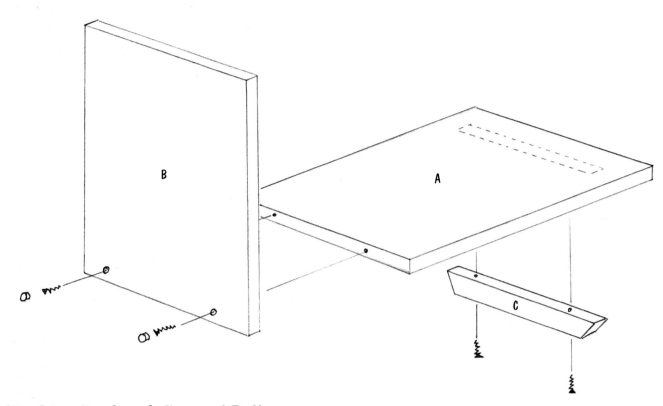

Desktop Bookrack Support Pattern

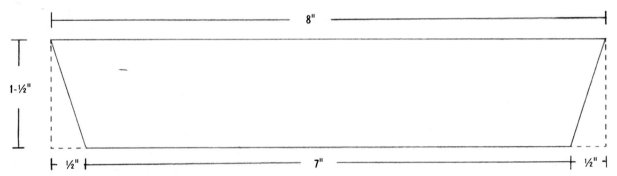

8"

1-½"

½"   7"   ½"

Desktop Bookrack Cut List

Overall dimensions: 15-¾" wide x 9-¼" deep x 12" tall

Ref	Qty.	Part	Stock	Thick	Width	Length
A	1	Bottom	Pine	¾"	9-¼"	15" (a)
B	1	Side	Pine	¾"	9-¼"	12" (a)
C	1	Support	Pine	¾"	1-½"	8" (b)

Notes

(a) Parts A and B are standard 1x10 pine, which actually measures ¾" thick by 9-¼" wide.

(b) Part C is standard 1x2 pine, which actually measures ¾" thick by 1-½" wide.

Additional Materials

Wood plugs (2 needed)

Photo 1 For a perfectly straight cut on the workpiece ends, a clamped-on guide ensures exact control of the jigsaw.

Photo 2 A block plane creates the bevel on the bookrack support foot.

Photo 3 With the support foot upside down in a vise, drill countersunk pilot holes for the attachment screws.

Photo 4 Clamp up the assembly until the glue dries.

Building the Bookrack

The bookrack consists of only two main parts – a bottom piece, and a side piece set at a right angle to the bottom. A narrow support foot attached underneath tilts the rack slightly to keep the books in place. Start by cutting the bottom and side pieces to length. Since this will be a plain butt joint, cut the joining edges very straight by using a clamped-on guide for a jigsaw to follow, as in Photo 1. A fine-cut blade will help make this a smooth, clean cut.

Cut the support foot from an 8" piece of standard 1x2 pine, marking an angled line ½" down from each end on one side as reflected in the Bookrack Support Pattern on Page 106, then cut off the corner on the line to create a slight taper on the ends.

This support foot attaches underneath the bookrack at a right angle, but because it tilts the rack the foot won't rest flat on a desktop. To correct this, create a slight bevel on the bottom of the foot by clamping it upside down in a vise and shaving off a small amount of wood from one edge with a block plane, as in Photo 2. This won't take much so go slowly, and check after each pass of the plane by removing the support foot from the vise and placing underneath the bookrack bottom piece to see how it rests on your bench or worksurface. You can see how this will look in the lead photo for this project. Since you won't be removing a lot of wood you could also create this bevel with a file, a sander or a sanding block.

When you have the bevel just right, place the support foot back in the vise and countersink two pilot holes through the bottom (Photo 3). We'll drive screws through these holes to attach the support foot.

Assemble the bookrack by applying glue to one end of the bottom piece, and clamping the side piece to this edge, as shown in Photo 4.

Photo 5 To keep the screws hidden in the finished bookrack, start by drilling countersunk pilot holes about ¼" deeper than normal.

Photo 6 Drive the screws home, setting them ¼" below the wood surface.

Photo 7 With a bit of glue in the countersink, tap in wooden plugs to hide the screw heads.

Photo 8 Trim off the excess plug, then sand everything smooth. Once painted, those plugs will disappear.

After the glue has thoroughly dried, remove the clamps and hang the assembly over the edge of a bench or other worksurface and clamp it in place, and then drill two countersunk pilot holes for reinforcing screws (Photo 5). Drill the countersinks deep enough for wooden plugs that will hide the screws entirely.

To do this, drill the countersink so the open portion at the top of the pilot hole is about ¼" deep. When you drive a pair of 1-⅝" or 1-¾" screws home, the screw heads won't be flush with the surface, but rather ¼" below it (Photo 6). Now, dab a small amount of glue around the inside of the countersink and tap in wood plugs to cover the screw heads (Photo 7). You don't have to pound these to death, just tap them in until firm and the glue will do the rest.

When the glue has dried, trim off the exposed portion of the wood plug. In Photo 8, I'm using a fine-cut pull-saw to neatly cut off the plug, but you could also use

a block plane or sharp chisel. Sand the plugs smooth and flush, then give the entire bookrack a sanding as needed with #100-grit followed by #150-grit paper. Pay particular attention to all edges when sanding, making sure to lightly smooth over all sharp corners and edges.

As an alternative to flush plugs you might consider wooden "button" plugs. These plugs have a rounded button-like top. You install them into a countersink the same way as flush plugs, but the button remains visible above the surface for a decorative touch that many people like.

To attach the support foot, first drive 2" screws into the countersunk holes until they poke out slightly, then press the foot in place on the underside of the bookrack 1" from the end and centered side-to-side. This will create two small marks where the screws will penetrate the bottom. Drill ⅛" pilot holes into the bottom on the marks, being careful to drill no deeper than ½" – mark the drill bit with masking tape to act as a stop guide.

Apply a small amount of glue to the mating surface of the support foot, place it on the underside of the rack and screw it securely into place (Photo 9).

You can apply the finish of your choice at this point. A bit of dark stain followed by satin or gloss polyurethane would look very nice, as would leaving the wood its natural color and using polyurethane, shellac or a spray lacquer. To complement the color of the room where I planned to use the bookrack, I've decided to paint it an almond color. I moved out into the yard to keep paint out of the house, and sprayed quick-drying acrylic enamel to finish the project (Photo 10). If you decide to go this route, be sure to cover your worksurface (in this case a small folding worktable I borrowed from my wife's office) with newspaper. When spraying, be mindful of the wind direction and apply the paint from the upwind side.

The paint I used was an all-in-one paint and primer, but if you choose regular paint it's a good idea to first give the bookrack a coat of primer. This will help the paint adhere better, and will do a better job of hiding the wood grain and any knots the wood may have. The type and brand of paint you use will determine how many coats you'll need to apply. I gave the rack three coats, which completely covered the wood grain and imparted a nice shine to the project.

And those screws covered by the plugs? Totally invisible.

Photo 9 Glue and screw the support foot about 1" from the bookrack's open end.

Photo 10 It's always a good idea to use spray paint and other aerosol finishes outdoors. Cover everything you don't want paint on.

Display Shelf

I'm betting that a lot of parents reading this are familiar with George Carlin's famous "Everybody needs a place for their stuff" routine. Not only is it hilarious, but it's absolutely true. While old George was speaking directly to adults, it's no less true that kids need a place for their stuff, too. And that's where this project comes in, with a display shelf they'll be proud to use to show off their most prized stuff. The best part is that this project is completely customizable – your kids can change the dimensions any way they want to accommodate whatever they want to display.

Display Shelf

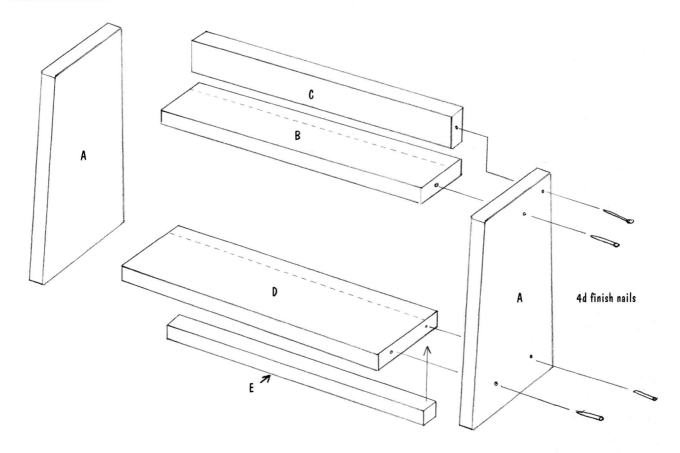

Display Shelf Side Pattern on next page

Display Shelf Cut List

Overall dimensions: 13-½" wide x 4-½" deep x 9-¼" tall

Ref	Qty.	Part	Stock	Thick	Width	Length
A	2	Sides	Pine	¾"	4-½"	9-¼"
B	1	Top Shelf	Pine	¾"	2-½"	12" (a)
C	1	Top Shelf Back	Pine	¾"	1-½"	12" (b)
D	1	Bottom Shelf	Pine	¾"	3-½"	12" (c)
E	1	Bottom Shelf Back	Pine	¾"	¾"	12" (d)

Notes

(a) Part B can be cut from standard 1x3 pine, which actually measures ¾" thick by 2-½" wide.

(b) Part C can be cut from standard 1x2 pine, which actually measures ¾" thick by 1-½" wide.

(c) Part D can be cut from standard 1x4 pine, which actually measures ¾" thick by 3-½" wide.

(d) Part E can be cut from any ¾" x ¾" square dowel, not just pine.

Additional Materials

Wood filler

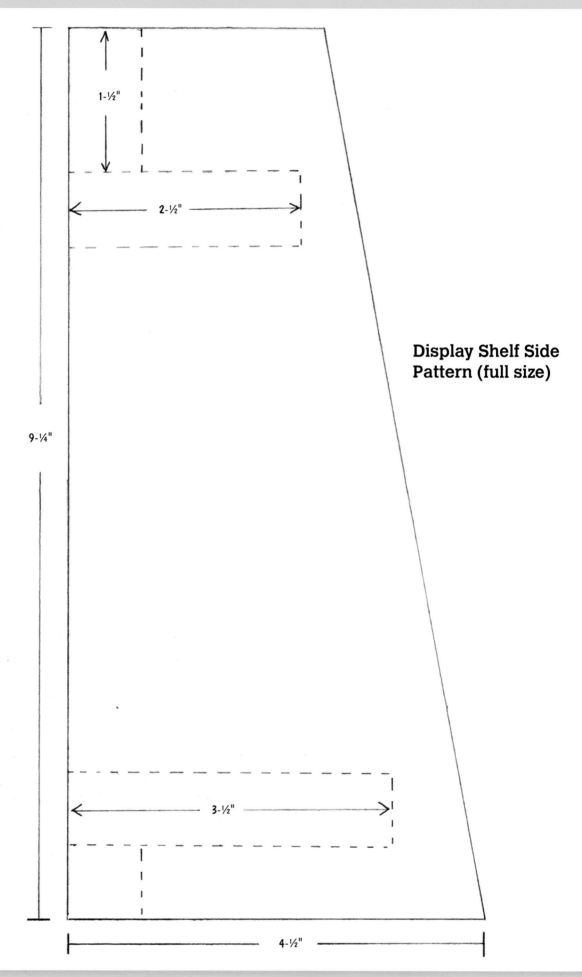

Display Shelf Side Pattern (full size)

1-½"

2-½"

9-¼"

3-½"

4-½"

Building the Display Shelf

Although the side pieces require an angled cut, the rest of this project is made entirely with off-the-rack wood in standard widths, so you'll only need to cut all other components to length. Begin by laying out the pattern for the display shelf sides from page 112 onto your stock (pattern also available for download at PopularWoodworking.com/HamlerBook). In Photo 1, you can see how I used a piece of 1x8 pine and laid out the side patterns front-to-front so I only had to make a single angled cut. Of course, you can use a piece of 1x6 and cut the patterns out end-to-end if you don't have a 1x8.

With the two sides cut out, tape them together like a pair of bookends to refine and smooth out the angled front edge, as shown in Photo 2. This is a good trick to use whenever you are creating workpieces in matched pairs. In this case, the double-wide taped workpieces were easy to hold square while sanding those front edges, and it cut the sanding time in half.

The shelves are different widths, but each is made the same way by edge-gluing two pieces of stock together to create an "L" shape, which has a couple of benefits. For the narrow top shelf, the second piece serves as a back to keep things from sliding off. The back piece on the wider lower shelf, meanwhile, lines everything up for a secure footing wherever you place the display shelf. These "L"-shaped shelf assemblies effortlessly keep everything square when putting the project together.

Create the top shelf by gluing the back piece to the top rear edge and clamping it up (Photo 3). The bottom shelf assembly goes together in the same way, but the back piece goes on the bottom side this time. Because these are long-grain to long-grain glue joints, they're plenty strong.

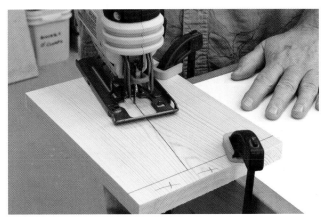

Photo 1 Both shelf sides can be cut from a single piece of 1x8 pine.

Photo 2 Taping the workpieces together makes sanding the edges easier and more uniform.

Photo 3 Assemble the shelves with glue and clamps, then allow to dry.

Photo 4 Carefully line up the shelf assemblies inside the two sides, then glue and clamp.

Photo 5 When the glue has dried, reinforce the display shelf with 4*d* finish nails and countersink them.

Photo 6 Touch up the nail holes and any other blemishes with wood filler.

Photo 7 When the wood filler has dried, sand smooth. Those spots will disappear when you paint the shelf.

When the glue has dried, unclamp the two shelf assemblies. Apply glue to the ends of both and place them between the two sides so the upper shelf aligns with the top of the two sides, while the lower shelf aligns with the bottom. You'll find this easy to do on a bench or other flat worksurface, as shown in Photo 4. Clamp up the complete unit till dry.

This display shelf uses butt joints, and while they would probably be fine for this usage, to be on the safe side let's reinforce them with a few nails. Unclamp the assembly and drive two 4*d* finish nails through the sides and into the ends of each shelf unit, then use a nail set to place the nail heads slightly below the surface of the wood (Photo 5).

It's not always necessary to hide nails – they'd probably not show that much if we stained and varnished this project – but I've decided to paint it instead. To prepare for painting let's hide the nail holes with wood filler, as in Photo 6. Back in Photo 4, you may have noticed a rather ugly knot on the one side. That would

show through paint, so I've filled it with the wood filler as well. Allow the filler to dry per package directions, then sand smooth. I used #150-grit to level that filler with the wood, and in Photo 7 you can see how both the nail holes and that pesky knot have been filled. Once painted, those will disappear.

Since I plan to use this display shelf in the same room as the Desktop Bookrack project (Page 105), I've elected to cover it with the same almond-colored spray paint. However, your kids may have other ideas for colors so let their imagination run free. The spray paint I used was both paint and primer in one, but if you use regular paint you'll want to brush or spray on a coat of primer first. Wood filler tends to soak up paint even more than bare wood does. Primer not only helps block soaking, but it goes a long way to hiding wood blemishes like that knot I had on one side.

Passive Speaker

Tablets and smart phones are great for storing and playing your favorite music, but the built-in speakers are terrible. It's not their fault really, since they sound about as good as possible for a speaker the size of a grain of rice. Unless you use headphones or an electronic speaker arrangement of some kind, you just don't get the enjoyment you're looking for. There is, however, a way to get better sound without electronics or batteries of any kind. It's called a passive speaker, and it works the same way a megaphone does.

Those tiny speakers on the bottom of your tablet or phone throw sound in all directions. A passive speaker takes the sound from the bottom and channels it in a single direction – forward – which immediately makes

it easier to hear in the same way a megaphone directs sound at a crowd. Meanwhile, the open space inside a passive speaker reflects the sound waves and reverberates to add depth and a feeling of spaciousness, the way the interior of a guitar does.

Wow, this is all pretty complicated, right? Well no, not at all. In fact, a homemade passive speaker like the one in this project is easy to build, and it'll reward you with fantastic sound. I've designed this speaker to work with my wife's iPad Mini, so all the measurements are specific to it, but adjusting it for other tablets or cell phones is as simple as adjusting the overall length and location of the inner channels. I'll address that at the end of the project.

Passive Speaker

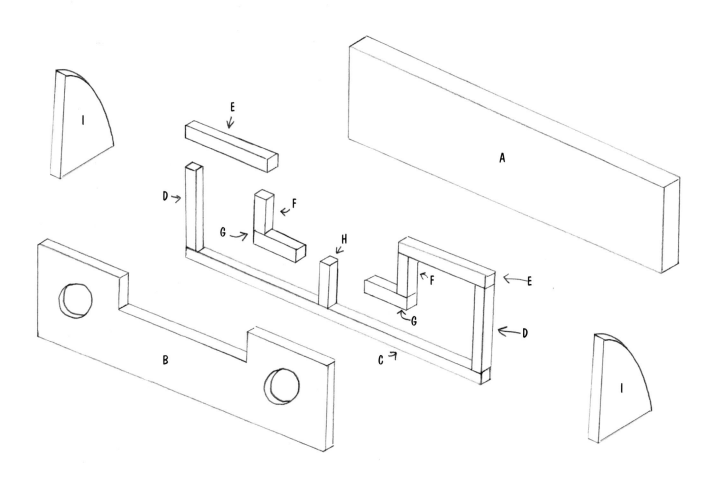

Passive Speaker Cut List

Overall dimensions: 13-½" long x 3" deep x 3-¾" tall (including supports)

Ref	Qty.	Part	Stock	Thick	Width	Length
A	1	Speaker Back	Oak	¾"	3-½"	12-½"
B	1	Speaker Front	Oak	½"	3-½"	12-½"
C	1	Bottom Spacer	Oak	½"	½"	12-½"
D	2	Side Spacers	Oak	½"	½"	2-½"
E	2	Top Spacers	Oak	½"	½"	3-½"
F	2	Center Side Spacers	Oak	½"	½"	2"
G	2	Center Bottom Spacers	Oak	½"	½"	1-½"
H	1	Center Divider Spacer	Oak	½"	½"	1"
I	2	Supports	Oak	½"	3"	3-¾"

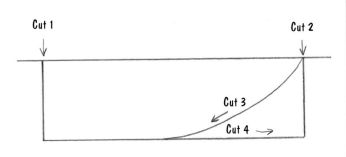

Photo 1 Cut a square opening with four cuts, as shown in this diagram.

Photo 2 Sandpaper wrapped around a wood block quickly squares and smooths the cut opening.

Photo 3 Clamp the speaker front to scrap and drill both speaker openings. A Forstner bit is perfect for this.

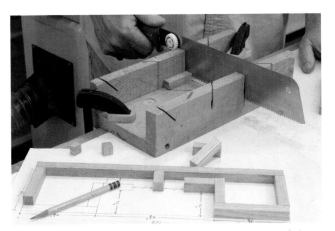

Photo 4 As you cut the spacers for the interior of the speaker, keep things in order by arranging them on the pattern.

Building the Passive Speaker

Begin by cutting the speaker front and back to size. The back is standard 1x4 oak, which actually measures ¾" thick; the front is ½" oak; both have standard widths of 3-½" so you'll only need to cut them to length. The speaker back is a simple rectangle, but the front features a cutout for the iPad. Mark the workpiece per the Speaker Front Pattern on Page 118, and cut the opening with a scroll saw, jigsaw or coping saw. To make those square corners you may find it easier to do it in four cuts, as shown in the diagram in Photo 1.

Wrap a piece of #100-grit sandpaper around a small wooden block and sand the opening square (Photo 2). Follow with #150- or #180-grit paper to nicely smooth the edges.

Mark the locations of the speaker holes per the Speaker Front Pattern, and use a 1-⅝" Forstner or spade bit to drill them out (Photo 3). Whichever bit you use, this is a pretty large diameter so it's a must to clamp the workpiece to a solid surface. Note here the piece of scrap under the workpiece to prevent tear-out on the underside and protect the benchtop.

The speaker is essentially a sandwich: a system of channels in between the solid front and back routes the sound to the chambers on either side. Create this by cutting spacers from standard 1/2" oak square dowel to the lengths shown on the Speaker Layout Guide on Page 118. Square ends are a must for these spacers, so a miter box and a fine-cut saw is your best bet (Photo 4). You might find it easier to keep track of all these small parts if you print out a full-size copy of the Layout Guide, and then set each of the spacers in its assigned spot on

Speaker Back Layout Guide (half size)

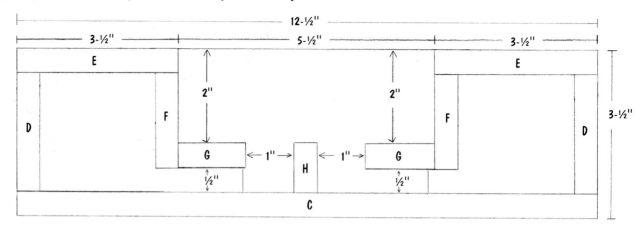

Speaker Front Pattern (half size)

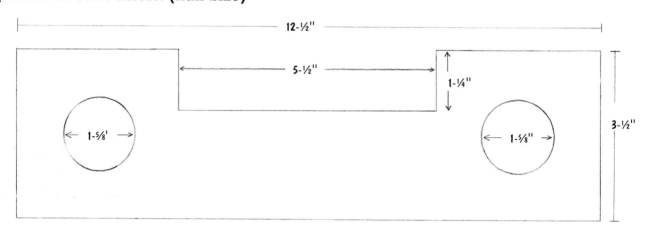

Speaker Support Pattern (full size)

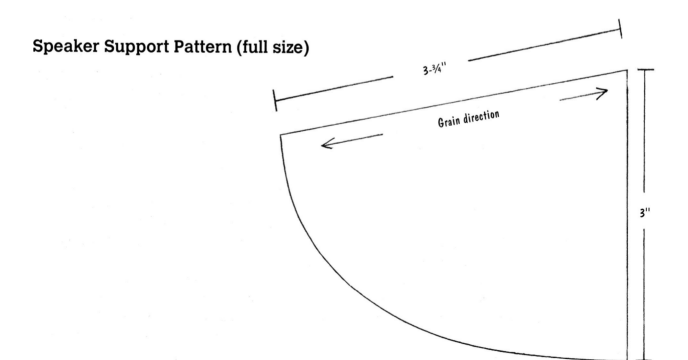

Grain direction

3-¾"

3"

Photo 5 Glue the spacers in place to form the inner sound channels.

Photo 6 With the spacers in place, clamp the front to complete the assembly.

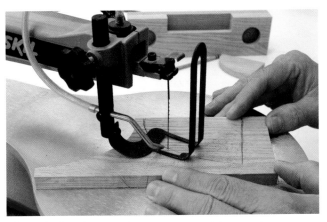

Photo 7 Cut the speaker supports with a coping saw or, as shown here, a scroll saw.

Photo 8 Tape the two supports together and sand both at the same time.

the pattern. (Patterns for this project are available for download at PopularWoodworking.com/HamlerBook).

Assembling the speaker is just a matter of gluing the spacers into their respective places on the speaker back, then gluing on the front to complete the sandwich (Photo 5). I've lettered the spacers in the best order to glue them into place, essentially from the bottom up. Start with the long Part C on the bottom, and then glue Parts D, E and so on in order on each side. Finish by gluing the single center divider into place.

Apply glue to the top surface of each spacer and put the speaker front in place, then clamp up the entire assembly to dry as shown in Photo 6. When dry, give the assembly a sanding with #100-grit, followed by higher grit as desired.

Transfer the pattern for the two speaker supports to ½" stock, then cut them out (Photo 7). These parts are too small to clamp up and cut with a jigsaw, so I'm using a scroll saw. You can also use a coping saw or, if you have one, a band saw.

I find it easier to sand edges of identical small parts by taping them together as in Photo 8, and doing them simultaneously. This gives a wider sanding area, which helps keep the sanding block square to the edges, and gets the job done in half the time. Start with #100-grit paper, followed by #150- or #180-grit. Repeat for the faces.

To attach the supports, place the speaker face down on your worksurface, apply a bit of glue to the mating surfaces, and clamp them to the assembly (Photo 9). The table surface automatically gets the supports flush on the speaker front, while placing a straight piece of scrap along the top edge aligns them with the speaker top.

When the assembly has dried, remove the clamps and apply the finish of your choice (Photo 10). I used a golden oak stain, but a darker walnut stain would also look great. Be sure to have your kids spread out newspaper and wear gloves when applying stain, as it makes a near-permanent mess of anything you get it on.

(Unlike me, it might also be a good idea not to wear a bright yellow shirt!) Apply the stain per manufacturer's directions, and when dry follow by brushing or spraying on a clear topcoat of shellac, polyurethane or lacquer.

Now, let's address customizing this passive speaker for your kids' devices. The speaker works when you place the device inside the opening, where the inner channels direct sound from the device speakers through the side chambers. You can see in Photos 11 and 12 how the channels in the project speaker match up with the bottom of the iPad Mini.

To customize this project to a particular device you'll need to change two things – the overall length and the center sound channels. The iPad Mini is 5-¼" wide, so I've sized the opening at 5-½" to give ⅛" clearance on each side, which is what I recommend you do as well. Have your kids measure their device and add ¼" (for ⅛" clearance on the sides), and that's the size of your opening. Shorten the length of Parts C and G accordingly to accommodate. For example, an iPhone 5 is about 2-¼" wide so you'd want the opening to be 2-½". That would shorten the overall length by 3".

The sound channels at the bottom should match the speakers on the bottom of your device. The iPad Mini has two internal stereo speakers, each ¾" long. I've sized the sound openings in the project speaker to reflect this – the 1" openings allow for the iPad to move ⅛" in each direction without blocking the internal speakers. Using an iPhone 5 as an example again, the speaker is about ½" long. Adding ⅛" to each side makes for a channel opening of ¾". Adjust yours accordingly.

Finally, although most tablets and cell phones offer stereo sound, some have only one speaker on the bottom located to one side or the other. If this is the case, simply eliminate the center divider (Part H), and make your speaker with a single opening at the bottom that channels the sound in both directions.

Photo 9 Line up the supports with the speaker top and front, then glue and clamp them into place.

Photo 10 A coat of stain brings out the beauty of the oak's grain.

Photo 11 This inside view shows the sound channel openings.

Photo 12 The iPad Mini has two speakers that fit over the sound channel openings inside the assembly.

Anything Box

I've always thought boxes were at the very heart of woodworking. So many aspects of crafting things from wood depend on the skills honed by making boxes. Think of just about anything made of wood, and you can see the roots of the box maker's craft. Kitchen cabinets? Boxes with doors. Drawers? Sliding boxes. Tables? Open boxes.

You get the idea. Several of the projects in this book are based on basic box construction: Gwen's Toolbox, the Cornhole Game, and Foosball, for example. But I wouldn't have considered this book complete without a true box project. The skills kids learn here will serve them well for just about anything else they make later in life.

Anything Box

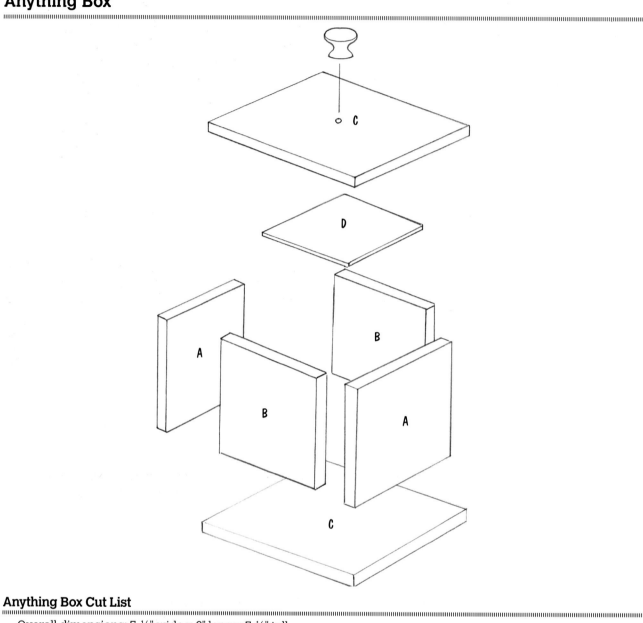

Anything Box Cut List

Overall dimensions: 5-½" wide x 6" long x 5-½" tall

Ref	Qty.	Part	Stock	Thick	Width	Length
A	2	Wide sides	Pine	¾"	4"	5-½" (a)
B	2	Narrow Sides	Pine	¾"	4"	3-½" (b)
C	2	Base/Lid	Pine	¾"	5-½"	6" (a)
D	1	Lid Keeper	Poplar	¼"	3-½"	4" (c)

Notes

(a) Parts A and C can be cut from standard 1x6 pine, which actually measures ¾" thick by 5-½" wide.

(b) Part B can be cut from standard 1x4 pine, which actually measures ¾" thick by 3-½" wide.

(c) Part D can be cut from standard ¼" x 4 poplar, which is a true ¼" thick, but 3-½" wide. You can use any ¼" material for this part.

Additional Materials

Handle or knob (1 needed)

Photo 1 Glue the narrow sides between the two wide sides to create the box body.

Photo 2 Clamp the box assembly until the glue dries.

Photo 3 Sanding the box on a sheet of sandpaper held to a flat surface cleans up the bottom edge to prepare for gluing the bottom into place.

Photo 4 Lightly trace pencil lines onto the bottom piece around the inside and outside of the box.

Building the Anything Box

Boxes can use a variety of joints, but in holding with the theme of this book, this design keeps things very simple. I've designed it to use standard 1-by lumber – pine in this case – so kids only need to cut components to length. To begin, cut each of the workpieces to size per the Cut List on Page 122, with a handsaw or jigsaw.

To give us strong long-grain to long-grain joints and a handsome appearance, assemble the body of the box with the wood grain oriented vertically. Apply glue to the edges of the narrow sides and place them between the two wide sides, as in Photo 1. Now, clamp up the assembly until the glue dries (Photo 2).

Remove the clamps and give the open-ended box a good sanding inside and out. This is easier now before the bottom is attached because you can reach right through the box with your sandpaper. To ensure that the bottom

of the box fits flush, you can run the box over a sheet of sandpaper held on a reliably flat surface, as shown in Photo 3. This makes a smooth mating surface for gluing, and removes any glue squeeze out from being clamped up. This is also a good time to sand both the bottom and lid.

We'll attach the box bottom with glue and nails. To prepare the bottom for mounting, center the box atop the bottom piece and trace around the box's inner and outer edges, as in Photo 4. Repeat this for the underside of the lid, but only trace around the inside of the box for this piece. You'll see why shortly. I'm making the pencil lines nice and dark for the photos, but make your marks as light as possible.

Clamp the box bottom to a piece of scrap to drill pilot holes for the nails. Use the traced outline as your guide to drill two holes in the tracing of the wide edges, and

Photo 5 Use your penciled lines to place pilot holes in the center of the traced outline.

Photo 6 Glue the bottom in place, then strengthen the joint with 4*d* finish nails.

Photo 7 Use a nail set to drive the nail heads slightly below the wood's surface.

Photo 8 Center the lid keeper underneath the lid, and glue it into place.

a single pilot hole in the narrow edges. In Photo 5, I've clipped the head off a 4*d* nail and am using it to drill the pilot holes.

Invert the box and apply glue on all four of the bottom edges. Set the bottom into place and drive 4*d* finish nails into your pilot holes (Photo 6). With the nails driven in, use a nail set to place their heads slightly below the surface of the wood (Photo 7). This will keep the nail heads from scratching the surface of whatever you set the box on. By the way, I've used six small nails here to secure the bottom, but if you prefer you can countersink four pilot holes through the bottom – one for each side of the box – and drive in 1-¼" screws instead. The choice is up to you and your young woodworker.

There are several ways to secure a box lid, but for a free lid like this one that will lift completely off the box, a lid keeper is easiest. This is simply a ¼"-thick piece of wood

the same size as the box interior, centered and attached to the underside of the lid. The keeper registers with the box opening, keeping the lid centered and in place.

Apply glue to one side of the keeper and place it on the underside of the lid inside the lines you traced earlier, as shown in Photo 8. Press the keeper into place and hold it for half a minute or so to give the glue a chance to grab, then clamp it in place until dry. I've used some leftover ¼"-thick poplar from the Trebuchet Project (Page 51) for the lid keeper, but you can use any wood you can find in a ¼" thickness.

You can leave the lid as is and just lift it off the completed box by its edges, but you'll find it nicer and more attractive to attach a small knob. Hold a ruler from corner-to-corner of the lid to find the center and mark it with a pencil, then drill a hole sized to fit the attachment

Photo 9 A simple cabinet knob adds a nice detail and makes it easy to remove the top.

Photo 10 A few coats of polyurethane varnish add a warm tone to the finished box.

screw of whatever knob you find. Slip the screw in from the underside of the lid, and then spin the knob into place (Photo 9).

Kids can finish this box any way they like – paint, stain, or appliqués or other decorations. This particular box is destined to reside on my kitchen counter, so I've chosen several coats of satin polyurethane varnish to protect it against the occasional splash. As you can see in Photo 10, poly darkens the pine to a deep amber hue that will look attractive in any setting.

This project is eminently customizable simply by changing the dimensions of the components. I've used ¾"

pine here, but any wood species in any thickness would also work well. If made without a lid, a box like this would be an excellent caddy for TV remotes. Speaking of the lid, instead of using a knob, you could choose a regular handle of the type found on drawers and cabinets, though it likely would require two mounting holes.

As always, encourage your young woodworkers to come up with their own ideas, then help turn them into reality.

Dragon Coin Bank

If it's big and scaly, it's a safe bet that kids love it, which probably explains why kids like dragons so much – you just don't get much bigger and scalier. Plus, the breathing-fire part is a huge bonus.

For this project we'll scale down the big – but keep all the fun – with a dragon coin bank they'll love to have in their room. There's not much to this one, just a main workpiece and two clear side pieces, plus a pair of eyes if you want, so this is a project that will go together quickly. And once kids build one, don't be surprised if they want to make more for friends and family.

Dragon Coin Bank

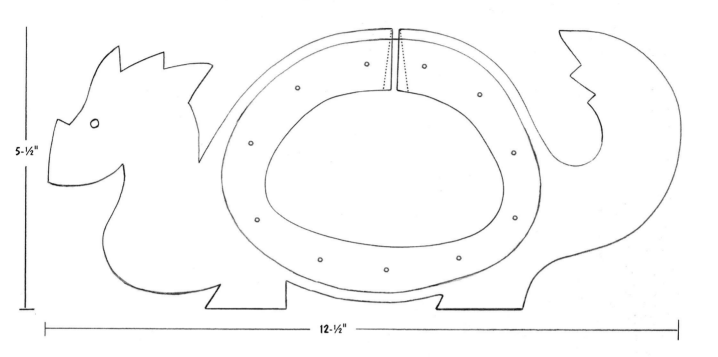

Dragon Coin Bank Cut List

Overall dimensions: 12-½" long x 1-¾" thick (including clear sides) x 5-½" tall

Ref	Qty.	Part	Stock	Thick	Width	Length
A	1	Main Body	Pine	1-½"	5-½"	12-½" (a)
B	2	Sides	Acrylic	⅛"	5-½"	6-½"

Notes

(a) Part A is standard 2x6 pine, which actually measures 1-½" thick by 5-½" wide.

Additional materials

#16 x ⅝" brass escutcheon pins (22 needed)

Optional – hardwood axles, trimmed for eyes (2 needed)

Building the Dragon Coin Bank

A piece of standard 2x6 pine construction lumber lies at the heart of this dragon, so let's start there. Cut a piece long enough to accommodate the 12-½" pattern; a length about 14" will do fine. Try to get wood that's nice and flat, but if it has a slight cupping to it you can flatten it out by running both sides back and forth over a piece of #80-grit sandpaper held on a reliably flat surface (Photo 1). This works very quickly for a workpiece with minor warping.

Base a pattern on the Dragon Pattern from Page 127 and transfer it to the workpiece. (A full-sized pattern is available for download at PopularWoodworking.com/ HamlerBook). In Photo 2 I've cut out the entire pattern, but if you prefer you can skip the cutting and tracing, and use spray adhesive to adhere the pattern directly to the wood as in the Fantasy Sword Project on Page 47. Either way, be sure to mark the eye location in the wood by poking an awl or nail through the pattern.

At 1-½" thick this workpiece isn't a good candidate for the jigsaw, because wood this thick can cause the blade to deflect on curved cuts, leading to uneven edges. I recommend a scroll saw, shown in Photo 3, or a coping saw to cut out the dragon shape. Pine construction lumber is soft, but you'll still need an aggressive scroll saw blade so be sure to check the packaging for stock thickness recommendations. Of course, if you have a band saw in your shop you may choose it to quickly handle this chore yourself.

For the project bank I've cut a straight coin slot, much like those found on traditional banks. Back in the old days they never made it easy to get that money out, although a bit of patience with a butter knife held in the slot would channel the coins out. However, you'll notice on the pattern that I've added optional cut lines to make a slot with angled sides that will funnel coins right through the opening when the bank is turned upside down. The choice is up to you and your young woodworker.

Give the finished cutout a good sanding, first with #100-grit and then #150-grit sandpaper. In Photo 4 I've rolled the paper up to get inside the tight curved portions. A spindle sander would make short work of this task if you have one, but it's not necessary.

Photo 1 Flatten the workpiece by sliding it over a piece of sandpaper held on a flat surface.

Photo 2 Copy and print out the pattern, and then attach or trace it onto one side of the workpiece.

Photo 3 Cut out the dragon shape on the scroll saw.

Photo 4 Give the workpiece a thorough sanding; a rolled-up piece of sandpaper reaches into the tight spots.

Photo 5 Cut the coin bank's two clear side pieces on the scroll saw, but leave the protective covering in place to prevent scratching.

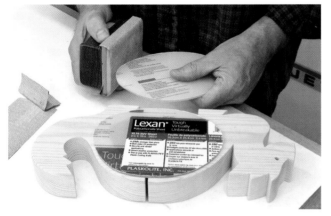

Photo 6 Sand off any burrs or sharp edges with a sanding block.

Photo 7 Trim the toy axles and glue them into the eye holes.

With the main workpiece complete, prepare the two clear sides for cutting by tracing the window shape from the pattern onto a ⅛" sheet of acrylic, polycarbonate or other strong plastic. Plastics of this type always come with a protective film on both sides. To prevent scratches to the plastic while you work, leave this film attached until just before nailing it in place.

Cut out the two clear sides with a coping saw or on the scroll saw (Photo 5). Cutting plastic materials almost always leaves a burr and sharp edges around the workpiece, but you can remove this quickly with a sanding block as in Photo 6.

Before attaching the clear sides, let's jump back to the main workpiece for a few final touches. To simulate the dragon's eyes all you need to do is drill a small hole all the way through the workpiece. But if you'd like to take it a step farther, use a couple of wooden toy axles for the

eyes instead. These come in several sizes, so you'll want to match the hole size to the axles you have.

Most available axles are a bit too long to use here – they'd bump together halfway – so trim most of the axle off with a pair of diagonal pliers. You only need a short length to insert into the holes so the amount you remove isn't critical. Put a drop of glue into the hole and insert the axles until flush, as in Photo 7. If the fit is really snug, tap them lightly into place with a hammer or mallet.

The last step for the main body is to apply the finish of your choice now, something you can't do after attaching the sides. For the project bank I've brushed on a couple coats of polyurethane, but quick-drying spray lacquer or shellac would speed things up. If you prefer, you can paint your dragon a good dragony color instead. And if you and your young woodworker are really ambitious, you can add scales and other details.

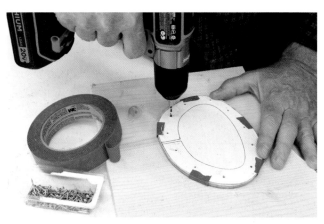

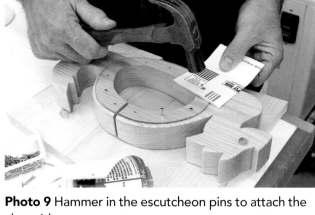

Photo 8 Stack the two clear side pieces and drill the pilot holes for the escutcheon pins.

Photo 9 Hammer in the escutcheon pins to attach the clear sides.

While the dragon's body is drying, drill the pilot holes in the clear sides. This is most easily done by stacking both pieces, and then cutting out the pattern and taping it to the stack, with the tape wrapped around the edges to keep everything aligned. Roll some tape loops and stick them to the underside of the stack so you can affix the stack to a piece of scrap to hold it for drilling. For the #16 escutcheon pins used here, use a ¹⁄₁₆" bit to drill the holes right through the pattern and into both side pieces at the same time (Photo 8).

Remove the tape and pattern, and peel off the protective plastic film from both side pieces. Working one side at a time, nail the clear sides into place. In Photo 9, you can see how I've protected the plastic from errant hammer blows. Take a piece of thin cardstock or stiff paper, fold it double, and punch a small hole in it. Place a pin into the pilot hole and slip the makeshift protector over the pin; this way if you or your child misses the mark, the folded card keeps the hammer from marring the plastic.

Once kids have mastered this dragon, the sky's the limit for bank styles. Patterns, outlines and shapes for any kind of animal – or any other object, really – are easy to find online or in coloring books. They can copy the pattern of their choice onto a suitably sized piece of wood, and they're in the banking business.

Train Whistle

Once upon a time train whistles were just that – whistles. They sounded with a harmonic tone that was simultaneously romantic and distant, and they seemed to tell a story of the road every time you heard one. These days trains don't have whistles, but loud, blaring horns that sound like nothing so much as an annoying 18-wheeler behind you in traffic. This project brings back the welcome sound of those old days with a bit of nostalgia that'll be appreciated by young and old alike.

This wooden whistle achieves that distinctive old-timey tone with a series of sounding holes of various length, drilled lengthwise into the workpiece. It's a little tricky, but if you take your time it's not difficult at all to make. Best of all, there's really only two workpieces – a length of standard pine 2x2 and a ½"-diameter dowel.

Train Whistle (full size)

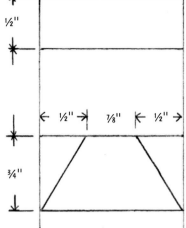

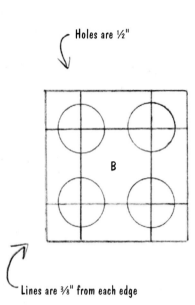

Holes are ½"

B

Lines are ⅜" from each edge

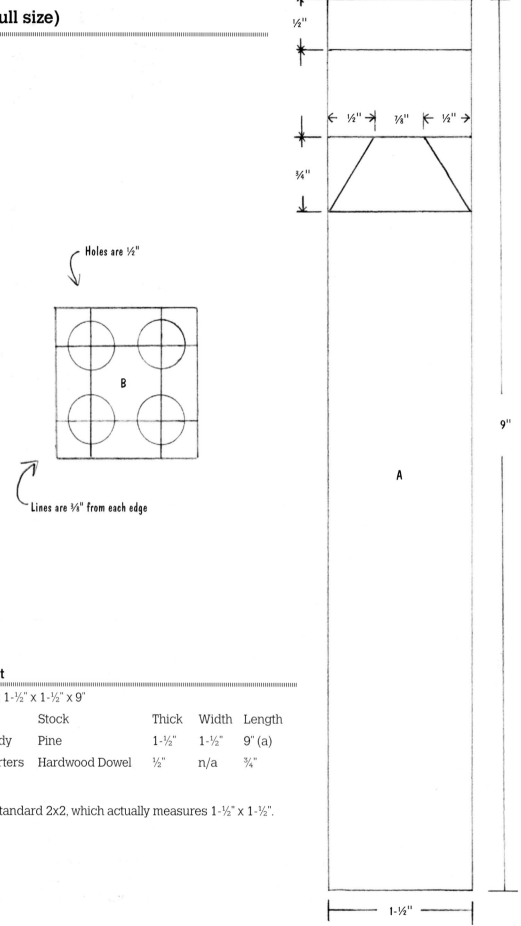

½"

½" ⅞" ½"

¾"

9"

A

1-½"

Train Whistle Cut List

Overall dimensions: 1-½" x 1-½" x 9"

Ref	Qty.	Part	Stock	Thick	Width	Length
A	1	Main Body	Pine	1-½"	1-½"	9" (a)
B	4	Air Diverters	Hardwood Dowel	½"	n/a	¾"

Notes

Main body is from standard 2x2, which actually measures 1-½" x 1-½".

Photo 1 Mark the end of the workpiece with a cut line, plus a distinctive mark to make it easy to reattach the piece later.

Photo 2 Cut off the end squarely to create the whistle mouthpiece. A fine-cut saw makes for a clean cut.

Photo 3 Lay out lines ⅜" from each edge to locate the drilling spots for the sound holes.

Photo 4 With the workpiece securely clamped and holding the drill squarely on the worksurface, drill four ½"-diameter starter holes.

Building the Train Whistle

Cut a 9" length of 2x2 (which really measures 1-½" x 1-½") by your preferred method. The secret of the melodic sound this whistle makes is four ½" holes drilled lengthwise inside the body, and to make those holes you'll need to remove a bit of the end. Use a square to measure and mark a cut line ½" from one end. This short end will become the mouthpiece, but before cutting it off mark the center of the cut line with an "X" so you can line it back up exactly when we glue it back on later (Photo 1).

Clamp the workpiece into a miter box and cut off the end. Since we want this to be an extremely clean cut to be reattached later, in Photo 2 I'm using a fine-cut pull-saw. However, any saw equipped with a fine-cut blade will do as long as you keep the cut square. Put the end piece aside in a safe spot where it won't get lost.

To line up the locations for the four holes, pencil a line squarely across the just-cut end, with each line ⅜" from

the workpiece sides (Photo 3). The four intersections of these lines is where you'll drill the four holes.

The drilling is tricky because the holes must extend directly down into the workpiece. If your shop boasts a drill press you may want to handle this task yourself there. However, here's how to drill those holes nice and straight without one.

Clamp the workpiece to a bench or other worksurface, then lay your drill flat on the bench with the tip of the drill bit against the workpiece. I got lucky, and the tip of the drill was at the perfect height to hit the drilling marks. If yours doesn't, you may need to shim either the drill or the workpiece with thin material – cardstock or thin plywood, for example – to hit your marks.

Once you have the drill bit matched to the drilling marks, slowly drill the two top holes to a depth of about an inch as in Photo 4. Then flip the workpiece over and drill the other two, also to a 1" depth. Drilling deep holes

Photo 5 Mark the bit with masking tape to indicate drilling depth for the first hole at 4".

Photo 6 Drill the sound holes to finished depth, relocating the tape each time.

on the side like this and keeping everything straight isn't easy, and the idea here is to establish four inch-deep starter holes, then transfer the workpiece to a vise and finish drilling the holes vertically

To achieve different tones, we'll drill the holes to depths of 4", 5", 6" and 7", so mark your drill bit with masking tape as a depth guide as shown in Photo 5. Drill the first hole with the bit marked to 4", then retape the drill bit for 5" and so on to drill the other three holes in turn (Photo 6).

Holes 6" and 7" deep are usually beyond the length of most ½"-diameter drill bits, although extra longs bits are available at your local home center or hardware store. However, on Page 12 I described how hex-shank drill bits can snap into drill extenders, and you'll find that a drill extender not only handles these deep holes but will be handy for other applications around the house and shop. You can see one in Photo 7, marked with masking tape for the deepest 7" hole.

Photo 7 A drill extension allows you drill holes deeper than the drill's actual length.

To cut the notched whistle openings, transfer cut lines as shown on the Whistle Pattern on Page 132. Support the workpiece at an angle by clamping it to a partially opened vise, then carefully cut out the triangular notches on the lines (Photo 8). A fine-cut saw or a fine blade installed in a coping saw is a must for this, although a band saw could handle the cuts quickly if you have one and want to take care of this task yourself.

Photo 8 Cut the whistle opening notches carefully; a fine-cut saw is best.

Photo 9 Remove ⅛" of material from a dowel to create the air diverters.

To create a whistle sound, an air diverter placed just over the whistle notches forces the air across the opening. The diverters are simply short ½" dowels with one side flattened. This is easiest to do by mounting a long dowel in a vise, or just clamping it to a bench, then planing or sanding ⅛" off the dowel to create the flat spot as shown in Photo 9. Once flattened, cut four ¾" lengths of dowel.

Dab a bit of glue inside the holes at the top of the whistle and slide the diverters into the holes so they're ⅛" below the top of the whistle (Photo 10). This will locate the bottoms of the diverters right at the top of the opening notches at the whistle's side. Note in Photo 10 how the diverters are oriented: the flat sides face the four corners, which lines the diverters up perfectly with the openings.

The last task is to create the whistle mouthpiece. Retrieve that ½" cut-off section from earlier, and draw pencil lines from corner to corner to locate its exact center. Now, clamp it to a piece of scrap and drill a ¾" hole through it on your center mark (Photo 11).

Apply glue to the top of the whistle, taking care not to get any down into the sound holes, and clamp the mouthpiece back in place atop the whistle as shown in Photo 12. Note here that I've lined it up with those marks created back in the first photo, so all the grain lines up perfectly.

Photo 10 Glue the air diverters into the sound holes ⅛" from the top.

Photo 11 Drill a ¾" hole through the mouthpiece section.

Photo 12 Line up your marks, then glue and clamp the mouthpiece back onto the workpiece.

Photo 13 When the glue dries, give all four sides a good sanding.

Photo 14 In this close-up, you can see how the air goes over the diverters.

When the glue has dried, remove the clamps and give the whistle a good sanding. In Photo 13, I'm running the whistle back and forth over a full sheet of #100-grit sandpaper on a flat surface. I then did the same thing with #150-grit paper, then I used a sanding block to nicely round all the edges.

To get an idea how the diverters work, take a look at Photo 14. The air goes into the edges of the four holes simultaneously, then down over the tops of the diverters (remember, they're recessed ⅛"). The air rushes down over the flat spots on the sides of the diverters and hits those triangular opening notches dead-on, which shoots the air out the sides. The air creates the sound as it goes over those notch openings, much like blowing over the top of a soda bottle. The depth of those internal holes determines the note each one makes – the deeper the hole, the deeper the note.

You can leave your whistle plain, but I gave mine a couple coats of spray shellac. The shellac gives the whistle a high-gloss sheen and protects it from getting dirty from lots of handling.

Candy Dispenser

It's an absolute truth that kids love candy. Even big kids like me. With that in mind, what could be better than a simple dispenser that gives you a perfect serving of your favorite candy every time you give it a simple pull? If there's anything better, I can't think of it.

This project is based on an age-old design that features a hopper full of candy – in this case, an inverted Mason jar – and a wooden slide underneath with a hole in it. With the slide fully inserted the candy falls into the hole.

Pulling the slide forward moves the hole out from under the dispenser top, while the solid rear portion of the slide blocks the hopper to keep the candy in. Enjoy, and repeat.

Before getting started you'll need to get a canning jar of the type that has an open lid rim that accepts a loose center insert. Leaving the insert out still allows the lid to be screwed on tightly, but it gives you an open-topped jar. I've used a one-pint canning jar here, but you can use any size jar you like.

Candy Dispenser

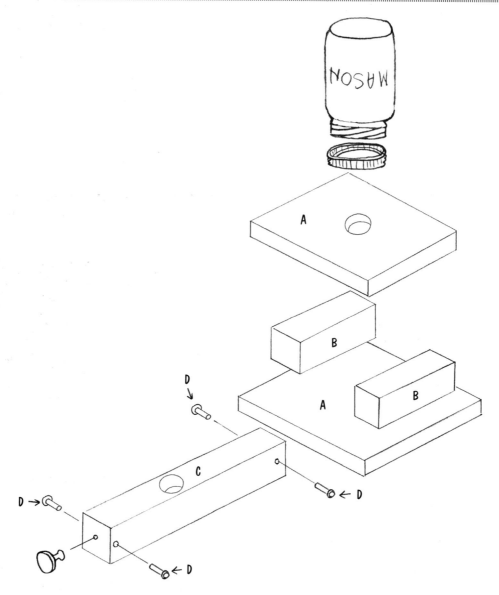

Candy Dispenser Cut List

Overall dimensions: 5-½ wide x 5-½" deep x 3" tall (not including jar)

Ref	Qty.	Part	Stock	Thick	Width	Length
A	2	Top/Bottom	Poplar	¾"	5-½"	5-½"
B	2	Sides	Poplar	1-½"	1-½"	4-½" (a)
C	1	Candy Slide	Poplar	1-½"	1-½"	9" (a)
D	4	Slide Stops	Hardwood Axle	⁷⁄₃₂"	n/a	n/a

Notes

(a) Parts B and C can be cut from standard 2x2 poplar, which actually measures 1-½" x 1-½"

Additional Materials

Canning jar with open-center lid (1 needed)

Pull knob (1 needed)

Candy (lots and lots needed)

Photo 1 Cut the two side components squarely with a handsaw and miter box.

Photo 2 Using a piece of the same material as a spacer, trace the outline of where the sides will fit onto the bottom.

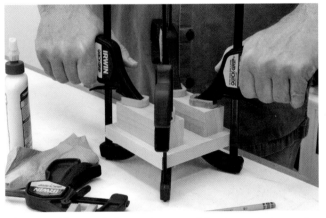

Photo 3 Glue and clamp the two sides into place on the bottom piece.

Photo 4 Drill a 1-¼" hole in the center of the dispenser top.

Building the Candy Dispenser

Cut the dispenser's base and top by your preferred method from any standard 1x6 material (actual measurement is ¾" x 5-½"). You can use pine if you want, though I've used denser poplar to lend a bit of extra weight and solidity. Set the top and base aside for now.

Use a handsaw and miter box to cut the two dispenser sides from 1-½" square material (Photo 1). Pine is fine and easy to work with, and you can use standard 2x2 construction lumber for your working stock if you like; 2x2 poplar is reliably 1-½" and unlike construction lumber has nice square edges. Sand the freshly cut pieces smooth with a sanding block and #100-grit sandpaper, followed by #150-grit.

To get a good sense of where to locate these two sides on the dispenser base, use another piece of 2x2 material as a spacer between them. Tear a couple small scraps of cardstock of the kind used for magazine inserts, slip them between the pieces and clamp them together. Center this atop the base and trace around it as in Photo 2. By using more of the same material from which we'll make the candy slide as the center spacer, we're sure to size that opening correctly. Those little slips of cardstock, meanwhile, will ensure a bit of extra room for the slide to move without binding.

Apply glue to the two sides and line them up with your tracing from earlier, and clamp them in place atop the dispenser base (Photo 3).

Mark the center of the dispenser top and drill a 1-¼" all the way through. In Photo 4 I'm using a Forstner bit, but a spade bit or small hole saw would also work well. As always, securely clamp the workpiece atop scrap to your bench or worktable.

Photo 5 Round over the edges of the top hole with a rotary tool, or by hand with rolled up sandpaper.

Photo 6 Adjust the fit of the candy slide by running it back and forth over a sheet of coarse sandpaper.

Photo 7 Trim a couple of toy axles and glue them in place to act as stops for the candy slide.

Photo 8 Put the slide into place, and then trace the location of the candy hole through the dispenser top.

Round over the edges of the hole you just drilled. You can do this with a small sanding drum and rotary tool as shown in Photo 5, or with a piece of rolled-up sandpaper. Now, apply glue to the top faces of the dispenser sides. Center and clamp the top in place to dry, and the dispenser base assembly is complete.

Cut the candy slide to length and give it a test fit in the dispenser base. Because we used some cardstock as spacers when locating the base sides, the slide should have room on the sides to fit without being too tight. However, there was no way to do the same for the top so chances are it'll be a bit snug. Adjust the fit by running the slide back and forth over coarse sandpaper and trying it again for size (Photo 6). Keep sanding until the slide moves freely in and out of the base; in fact, a little bit of wiggle room all around is good. When the fit is just right, give the slide a final sanding with #150-grit.

To capture the slide inside the dispenser base and prevent it from coming all the way out and spilling candy everywhere, you'll need to install a set of stops at each end. Drill a 7/32" hole about 1/4" from each end of the slide to accept a pair of hardwood toy axles. Right from the package the axles are a bit too long so clip them shorter with a pair of diagonal cutters. Put a dab of glue inside the front hole only, and slide in a pair of trimmed axles (Photo 7). This will be the front of the candy slide. Do not put the rear stops in yet, because we'll need to insert and remove the slide a few more times before we finish.

By the way, I've used the same hardwood toy axles here that have appeared in several of the projects because I had a supply of them in my shop. You can use short lengths of regular dowels instead, however. Just match the hole size to the dowel size, and glue them into place.

To locate the spot for the candy hole in the slide, insert it into the dispenser base until it stops firmly against the front. Now, trace through the hole in the top to mark the slide as shown in Photo 8. Use a 1-¼" Forstner or spade bit to drill a 1"-deep hole on your mark. This hole will rest right under the one in the top.

You can leave your candy dispenser plain, of course, but if you plan to finish or paint it, before final assembly is the time to do it. Once the slide is permanently installed in the base, you won't be able to apply finish. I chose a few coats of satin polyurethane varnish and let everything dry for a few days before proceeding. By the way, all modern finishes are food-safe once cured so there are no issues there. Just be sure your finish is fully cured before filling the dispenser with candy. Sniff it to see – if you can smell any trace of finish, it's not yet cured.

To prepare the jar for mounting, drill four evenly spaced pilot holes through the lid rim using a ¹⁄₁₆" bit (Photo 9). As before, I've clamped the work to a scrap board atop my worktable. Note that you'll need to rotate and reclamp the jar lid to drill all the holes.

Now, how do you want your jar to look when it's in place? If you're using a plain round jar with no obvious front you can attach the jar lid in any orientation. Most canning jars, however, are square and have an obvious front with an embossed logo. If you want this portion of the jar to face forward, screw the lid on and mark it so you know where the front of the jar will be. I used a fine Sharpie marker because it will rub right off later with a small bit of mineral spirits on a rag. I also put a small arrow on the center/front of the base with a piece of masking tape.

Center the lid upside down on the top of the dispenser base, aligning your marks, and secure it with four ⅝" nails. Hammering nails so close to the jar lid's side was difficult, so in Photo 10 I'm using a nail set to place them.

Finally, slip the candy slide into place and glue in the rear stops on each side of the back end of the slide.

All that's left to do now is fill the jar with your favorite candy, invert the dispenser base atop the jar, and screw it into place. Turn the dispenser right side up, and it's ready for use.

Because of my dedication to the project's success I did some exhaustive research to be sure of which candies were good choices, and I found that hard-shelled candy works best. Skittles, M&Ms, Good & Plenty, Reese's

Photo 9 Clamp the jar lid down and carefully drill ¹⁄₁₆" mounting holes through its rim.

Photo 10 Use a nail set to drive ⅝" nails to secure the inverted jar lid in the center of the dispenser top.

Pieces and similar candies all work well. Gummy bears, not so much.

To make sure my research was as thorough as possible, I think I went through three whole bags of candy to satisfactorily complete the testing.

About the Author

Originally a broadcast professional, A.J. Hamler has been a writer and editor for more than two decades, primarily in the areas of woodworking and home improvement. Hamler's articles have appeared in most of the woodworking and home-handyman magazines in the field, while his most recent books include "Birdhouses and More" (Popular Woodworking Books, 2014) and "Civil War Woodworking Volume II" (Linden Publishing, 2014). He also served as editor of "The Collins Complete Woodworker" (HarperCollins/Smithsonian, 2007), and wrote the shooting script for the DVD "Plumbing Projects 1-2-3" (Home Depot, 2008). Not all of Hamler's work is nonfiction – writing as "A.J. Austin," he has published two science-fiction novels and numerous short stories. When not in his workshop or fixing something around the house, Hamler enjoys Civil War re-enacting, gourmet cooking, and performing as a stage and voice-over actor.

Dedication

To Mom and Mike, who built things with me.
To my daughter Courtney, who I built things with.
And to my grandson Jed, who will one day build
things with skills handed down from all of us.

Build It with Dad

Build It with Dad. Copyright © 2015 by A.J. Hamler. Printed and bound in the United States of America. All rights reserved. No part of this book may be reproduced in any form or by any electronic or mechanical means including information storage and retrieval systems without permission in writing from the publisher, except by a reviewer, who may quote brief passages in a review. Published by Popular Woodworking Books, an imprint of F+W, A Content + eCommerce Company, 10151 Carver Rd. Blue Ash, Ohio, 45242. First edition.

a content + ecommerce company

Distributed in Canada by Fraser Direct
100 Armstrong Avenue
Georgetown, Ontario L7G 5S4
Canada
Tel: (905) 877-4411

Distributed in the U.K. and Europe by
F&W Media International, LTD
Brunel House, Ford Close
Newton Abbot
Devon TQ12 4PU, UK
Tel: (+44) 1626 323200; Fax: (+44) 1626 323319
Email: enquiries@fwmedia.com

Distributed in Australia by Capricorn Link
P.O. Box 704
Windsor, NSW 2756
Australia
Tel: (02) 4560-1600

Visit our website at popularwoodworking.com or our consumer website at shopwoodworking.com for more woodworking information.

Other fine Popular Woodworking Books are available from your local bookstore or direct from the publisher.

ISBN-13: 978-1-4403-3896-0

19   18   17   16   15   5   4   3   2   1

Editors: John Kelsey and Scott Francis
Designer: Laura Kagemann
Production Coordinator: Debbie Thomas

Read This Important Safety Notice

To prevent accidents, keep safety in mind while you work. Use the safety guards installed on power equipment. When working on power equipment, keep fingers away from saw blades, wear safety goggles to prevent injuries from flying wood chips and sawdust, wear hearing protection and consider installing a dust vacuum to reduce the amount of airborne sawdust in your woodshop. Don't wear loose clothing or jewelry when working on power equipment. Tie back long hair to prevent it from getting caught in your equipment. People who are sensitive to certain chemicals should check the chemical content of any product before using it. The authors and editors who compiled this book have tried to make the contents as accurate and correct as possible. Plans, illustrations, photographs and text have been carefully checked. All instructions, plans and projects should be carefully read, studied and understood before beginning construction. Due to the variability of local conditions, construction materials, skill levels, etc., neither the author nor Popular Woodworking Books assumes any responsibility for any accidents, injuries, damages or other losses incurred resulting from the material presented in this book. Prices listed for supplies and equipment were current at the time of publication and are subject to change.

Metric Conversion Chart

To convert	to	multiply by
Inches	Centimeters	2.54
Centimeters	Inches	0.4
Feet	Centimeters	30.5
Centimeters	Feet	0.03
Yards	Meters	0.9
Meters	Yards	1.1

Ideas · Instruction · Inspiration

These are other great Popular Woodworking products are available at your local bookstore, woodworking store or online supplier.

Popular Woodworking Magazine

Get must-build projects, information on tools (both hand and power) and their use and technique instruction in every issue of *Popular Woodworking Magazine*. Each issue (7 per year) includes articles and expert information from some of the best-known names in woodworking. Subscribe today at popularwoodworking.com.

Subscription • 7 issues/year

Getting Started With Routers

By David Thiel

The router is a fairly simple woodworking tool that is, conversely, the most versatile woodworking tool in any shop. This video will help you choose the correct router (or routers) to best fit the type of woodworking done in your shop, as well as provide the basic information to start you using routers freehand and in a router table.

Available at Shopwoodworking.com
DVD & download

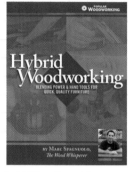

Hybrid Woodworking

By Marc Spagnuolo

Known online as The Wood Whisperer, Marc Spagnuolo presents a fresh approach to woodworking and furniture making by showing the most efficient ways to utilize both power tools and hand tools in the furniture building process. Not only will you learn which tools are best for which tasks, but you will also find tips for how to use, maintain, and fine tune them.

Paperback • 192 pages

Ultimate Workshop Solutions

By Popular Woodworking Editors

From better clamp storage, to the perfect miter saw stand to benches and beyond, you'll find 35 projects specifically designed to improve and organize your favorite space. These projects have been created by the editors of *Popular Woodworking Magazine* for your shop, and now we're pleased to share them with you.

Paperback • 192 pages

I Can Do That! Woodworking Projects, 2nd Edition

By Editors of Popular Woodworking

This book will show you how to build 38 quality furniture projects that can be completed by any woodworker with a modest (but decent) kit of tools in less than two days of shop time, and using raw materials that are available at any home center. The enclosed tool manual explains all the tools and shows you how to perform the basic operations in a step-by-step format.

Paperback • 176 pages

The Weekend Woodworker's Project Collection

By Editors of Popular Woodworking

This book has 40 projects from which to choose and, depending on the level of your woodworking skills, any of them can be completed in one or two weekends. Projects include: a game box, a jewelry box, several styles of bookcases and shelves, 5 mirror/picture frames and more. So, pick a project and get started – time's a wastin'!

Paperback • 256 pages

Furniture Fundamentals: Making Tables

Edited by Robert W. Lang

Features step-by-step photos and instruction, plus measured drawings, for 17 tables in a wide range of styles and skill levels. From simple tapered legs to contemporary cabrioles, from simple slab tops to draw-leaf tops, from side tables to game tables, you'll learn the techniques, tools and joinery necessary to build great-looking tables for every room in your house.

Paperback • 128 pages

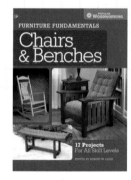

Furniture Fundamentals: Chairs & Benches

Edited by Robert W. Lang

Inside, you'll find step-by-step photos and instruction, plus measured drawings, for 17 seating projects in a wide range of styles and skill levels. Projects range from simple, square stools to more challenging chairs and benches with compound joints. You'll learn how to use the best tools for the job to cut all types of must-know chair joinery, simple turning techniques, upholstery and more.

Paperback • 128 pages

Visit **popularwoodworking.com** to see more woodworking information by the experts, learn about our digital subscription and sign up to receive our free newsletter or blog posts.